Using the
**Common Core
State Standards** for
Mathematics
With Gifted and
Advanced Learners

Using the
Common Core
State Standards for
Mathematics
With Gifted and
Advanced Learners

Edited by
Susan K. Johnsen, Ph.D.,
and Linda J. Sheffield, Ph.D.

Contributing Authors
Linda J. Sheffield, Ph.D. • Cheryll M. Adams, Ph.D.
Susan K. Johnsen, Ph.D. • Alicia Cotabish, Ed.D.
Joyce VanTassel-Baska, Ed.D. • Chrystyna V. Mursky, Ph.D.

Copublished With

 NATIONAL ASSOCIATION FOR **Gifted Children**

NCSM | LEADERSHIP IN MATHEMATICS EDUCATION NETWORK COMMUNICATE SUPPORT MOTIVATE

 NCTM | NATIONAL COUNCIL OF TEACHERS OF MATHEMATICS

PRUFROCK PRESS INC.
WACO, TEXAS

Prufrock Press Inc.
P.O. Box 8813
Waco, TX 76714-8813
Phone: (800) 998-2208
Fax: (800) 240-0333
http://www.prufrock.com

Table of Contents

Foreword

In the fall of 2011, at the annual retreat of the Board of Directors of the National Association for Gifted Children, an urgent request for guidance about the Common Core State Standards (CCSS) and their relationship to gifted programming and curriculum was heard from every corner of the membership. NAGC leaders and experts responded, starting with a meeting of the NAGC Association Editor, co-chairs of the Professional Standards Committee, the chair of the Education Committee, and the NAGC President and Executive Director at the 2011 annual convention in New Orleans. An ambitious plan was developed to address the needs of gifted education specialists and teachers regarding how to integrate the CCSS with their current programming and curricula.

Out of that meeting came the idea to develop two booklets, one on the Common Core State Standards for English Language Arts and one on the Common Core State Standards for Mathematics. All involved shared a heartfelt sense of urgency about the importance of this task. The Professional Standards Committee went to work immediately, spending evenings at the conference crafting initial informational materials on the CCSS to distribute via the NAGC website.

The Common Core State Standards are a significant milestone affecting education in the United States. As of this printing, 45 states have adopted the CCSS, attesting to the collective concern about the quality of education in our nation and the commitment to improve it. The CCSS embody significantly higher expectations for learning and thus, if implemented with fidelity, have the potential to dramatically alter achievement for all students.

Gifted educators are excited about the CCSS, as they reflect many of the strategies that the field of gifted education has been stressing for decades as important to deep learning and engagement and high achievement—high-level, analytical thinking and advanced problem-solving skills. However, the CCSS alone will not ensure that gifted children receive the advanced content, accelerative options, and high-level enrichment that they need to be challenged and make continuous progress in their areas of talent. Hence the need for these booklets: They will help educators understand how to use the CCSS as a foundation and go beyond them for those learners who meet the standards earlier and faster. The booklets also assist educators in coupling and integrating the CCSS with gifted education curricula, instructional practices, and program models. These booklets are a valuable resource for all educators, not just those who work specifically in gifted programs. The reality is that most gifted children receive their instruction from teachers in heterogeneous classrooms, and these booklets can help all educators differentiate content and instruction for high-ability learners.

I want to thank the members of the Professional Standards Committee and others, who worked diligently to respond so quickly to the needs expressed by NAGC members and to fast track the production of these booklets through their efforts in New Orleans and at a work weekend in February 2012, particularly co-chairs Joyce VanTassel-Baska and Susan Johnsen, Cheryll Adams, Rima Binder, Alicia Cotabish, Reva Friedman-Nimz,

Claire Hughes, Jennifer Jolly, Bill Keilty, Todd Kettler, Wayne Lord, Chrystyna Mursky, Julia Roberts, Elizabeth Shaunessy, Linda Sheffield, and Debra Troxclair. I also want to thank the NAGC staff members who edited and assisted with the production aspects of this project, especially Jane Clarenbach.

Paula Olszewski-Kubilius
NAGC President
2011–2013

Preface

The importance of strong curriculum in content areas for advanced learners is a basic consideration in all gifted programs nationwide. In no areas is this more needed than in English language arts and mathematics, as they constitute the cornerstones of learning in our schools at all stages of development. They also constitute important talent domains for the development of future professionals whose work is centered on the application of these subject areas.

Gifted education, through the National Association for Gifted Children (NAGC), has developed a set of curriculum, assessment, and learning environment standards for pre-K–grade 12 programs that promote careful curriculum planning, differentiated instructional approaches, and authentic learning assessments, all aspects of the work associated with the new Common Core State Standards (CCSS). However, it was clear to the Professional Standards Committee within the organization that the Gifted Programming Standards needed to be aligned to the new Common Core State Standards to ensure that the CCSS are appropriately adapted and differentiated for our best learners.

The group has worked over the past several months to draft two guides (one in English language arts and one in mathematics) for practitioners that provide such translations for use in an array of settings that contain advanced learners—from cluster-grouped classrooms to pull-out programs to special classes to special schools. The guides provide examples of the relevant CCSS, matched to a suggested activity for typical learners and then differentiated for advanced learners. Assessment examples are also provided, including appropriate rubrics. Related material on further alignment to 21st century skills, to collaboration for interdisciplinary adaptations, and to professional development are included for easy referencing.

We sincerely hope these booklets will be used to ensure that advanced learners experience a rich and challenging curriculum as a result of the new CCSS and that practitioners use the examples as a model for their own continued curriculum work on behalf of advanced learners.

Joyce VanTassel-Baska, Ed.D., and Susan K. Johnsen, Ph.D.
Co-Chairs
Professional Standards Committee
National Association for Gifted Children

Acknowledgments

From concept to publication, there are a number of experts in mathematics, curriculum, pedagogy, and standards who volunteered their time and energy to support the development of this book. We value all of the contributions, but we would be remiss if we did not mention key participants from different stages of the book's creation.

First, we acknowledge the leadership of NAGC president Paula Olszewski-Kubilius, who, in response to emerging calls for assistance from NAGC members, made this book a priority for the organization. We naturally turned to our colleagues on the NAGC Professional Standards Committee and other experts involved in gifted education standards for assistance. These volunteers helped develop the Common Core State Standards materials at the 2011 NAGC convention in New Orleans that provided an initial framework for these books.

Recognizing that publications are strengthened through a rigorous review process, we also want to thank the reviewers who took time to provide valuable advice and feedback: Susan Assouline, Linda Brody, Scott Chamberlain, Kathy Gavin, Ann Lupkowski-Shoplik, Sara Moore, and Janet Tassell. We also appreciate the comments on the manuscript that we received from the Council of State Directors of Programs for the Gifted. All of the suggestions helped shape the final books.

Finally, there are others who have supported the development process, the content, and the need for the book. We thank Nancy Green and Jane Clarenbach at the NAGC national office, NAGC Association Editor Sidney Moon, and Joel McIntosh and Jennifer Robins at Prufrock Press. We also thank our copublishers, the National Council of Math Supervisors and the National Council of Teachers of Mathematics.

Introduction

The purpose of this booklet is to provide classroom teachers and administrators with examples and strategies to implement the new Common Core State Standards (CCSS) for Mathematics for advanced learners at all stages of development in K–12 schools. One aspect of fulfilling that purpose is to clarify what advanced opportunities look like for such learners from primary through secondary grade levels. Specifically, how is effective differentiation designed for top learners in mathematics? How can educators provide the appropriate level of rigor and relevance within the new standards as they translate them into experiences for gifted learners? How can educators provide creative and innovative opportunities to learn that will nurture the thinking, reasoning, problem solving, passion, and inventiveness of our best students in mathematics?

In this booklet, trajectories for talent development in mathematics will be described. These progressions lend vision to the work of teachers as they deliver classroom instruction at one level and prepare students for succeeding levels in the journey toward self-fulfillment and the real world of science, technology, engineering, and mathematics (STEM) professions. What are the skills, habits of mind, and attitudes toward learning needed to reach high levels of competency and creative production in mathematics fields? How does the pathway from novice to expert differ among promising learners?

The booklet also includes multiple resources in the appendix material to support educators in developing and modifying materials for students who are advanced in mathematics. In addition to including a list of definitions of the key terms used in the booklet (Appendix A), we have included a research base of best practices in gifted education (Appendix B), annotated references to key publications and websites focused on mathematical creativity and giftedness (Appendix C), and a list of publications addressing mathematics and K–12 students (Appendix D).

The booklet is also based on a set of underlying assumptions about the constructs of giftedness and talent development that underpin the thinking that spawned this work. These assumptions are:

- Giftedness is developed over time through the interaction of potential with nurturing environmental conditions. The process is developmental, dynamic, and malleable.
- Many learners show preferences for particular subject matter early and continue to select learning opportunities that match their predispositions if they are provided with opportunities to do so. For many children, especially those in poverty, schools are the primary source for relevant opportunities to develop domain-specific potential, although markers of talent development also emerge from work done outside of school in co-curricular or extracurricular contexts.
- Aptitudes and interests may also emerge as a result of exposure to high-level, engaging, and challenging activities. Teachers should consider using advanced learning activities and techniques as a stimulus for all learners.
- Intellectual, cultural, and learning diversity among learners may account for different rates of learning, different areas of aptitude, different cognitive styles, and different

experiential backgrounds. Working with such diversity in the classroom requires teachers to differentiate and customize curriculum and instruction, always working to provide an optimal match between the learner and her readiness to encounter the next level of challenge.

Users of this booklet should note that the ideas contained herein are not intended to apply exclusively to identified gifted students; they also apply to students with potential in mathematics, as they also might develop motivation and readiness to learn within the domain of mathematics.

Finally, it is our hope that this booklet provides a roadmap for meaningful national, state, and local educational reform that elevates learning in mathematics to higher levels of passion, proficiency, and creativity for gifted—and, indeed, all—learners.

The Common Core State Standards

The Common Core State Standards for Mathematics are K–12 standards that illustrate the curriculum emphases needed for students to develop the skills and concepts required for the 21st century. Two sets of standards are described: Standards for Mathematical Practice and Standards for Mathematical Content. Adopted by 45 states to date, the CCSS are organized into key content domains and articulated across all years of schooling and, when adopted, replace the existing state content standards. The initiative has been state-based and coordinated by the National Governors Association (NGA) and the Council of Chief State School Officers (CCSSO). Designed by teachers, administrators, and content experts, the CCSS are intended to prepare K–12 students for college and the workplace.

The new CCSS are evidence-based, aligned with expectations for success in college and the workplace, and informed by the successes and failures of the current standards and international competition demands. The new standards stress rigor, depth, clarity, and coherence, drawing from national and international studies such as the National Assessment of Educational Progress (NAEP) Frameworks in Mathematics (NAEP, 2011) and the Trends in International Mathematics and Science Study (TIMSS) report in mathematics (National Center for Education Statistics [NCES], 2007). They provide a framework for curriculum development work. States are working within and across local districts to design relevant curriculum, align current practice to the new standards, and develop resources that support teaching and learning.

Rationale for the Work

The adoption of the Common Core State Standards in almost every state is cause for gifted education as a field to reflect on its role in supporting gifted and high-potential learners appropriately in the content areas. The field of gifted education has not always differentiated systematically in the core domains of learning, but rather has focused on interdisciplinary concepts, higher level skills, and problem solving, typically across domains. With the new CCSS and their national focus, it becomes critical to show how to differentiate for gifted learners within a set of standards that are reasonably rigorous in each subject area.

Some advocates of the new CCSS have suggested that the standards are already at such a high level that no specialized services and differentiation are needed for gifted students. Although the standards are strong, they are not sufficiently advanced to accommodate the needs of most learners who are gifted in mathematics. As the CCSS developers have noted, some students will traverse the standards before the end of high school (NGA & CCSSO, 2010b, p. 80), which will require educators to provide advanced content for them. In addition to the need for accelerative methods, there is also a need to enrich and extend the standards by ensuring that there are open-ended opportunities to meet the standards through multiple pathways; more complex, creative, and innovative thinking applications; and real-world problem-solving contexts. This requires a deliberate strategy among gifted educators to ensure that the CCSS are translated in a way that allows for differentiated practices to be employed with gifted and high-potential students.

As with all standards, new assessments will likely drive the instructional process. As a field, educators of the gifted must be aware of the need to differentiate assessments that align with the CCSS and content as well. Gifted learners will need to be assessed through performance-based and portfolio techniques that are based on higher level learning outcomes and that often vary from the more traditional assessments the CCSS may employ.

Although the new CCSS appear to be a positive movement for all of education, it is important to be mindful of the ongoing need to differentiate appropriately for top learners. As a field, it is also critical to agree on the need to align with this work so gifted education voices are at the table as the CCSS become one important basis, along with the newly revised InTASC Model Teacher Standards (CCSSO, 2011), for elevating teacher quality and student learning nationwide.

The Common Core State Standards for Mathematics have significant implications for teaching mathematics in grades K–12. Our collective future lies in the individual development of students with mathematical promise, students who will fulfill their own potential and also provide leadership for others. This individualized developmental approach includes students who traditionally have been identified as gifted, talented, advanced, or precocious in mathematics, as well as those students of promise who may have been excluded from the rich opportunities that might accompany this recognition. As with all students, these students with special needs deserve a learning environment that supports them in the fulfillment of their personal potential.

Alignment to 21st Century Skills

This booklet includes a major emphasis on key 21st century skills (Partnership for 21st Century Skills, n.d.) in overall orientation as well as in activities and assessments employed in the examples. Several of these skill sets overlap with the differentiation emphases discussed below in relation to the gifted standards. The skills receiving major emphases include:

- *Collaboration:* Students are encouraged to work in dyads and small groups of four to carry out many activities and projects, to pose and solve problems, and to plan presentations.
- *Communication:* Students are encouraged to develop communication skills in written, oral, visual, and technological modes in a balanced format within each unit of study.
- *Critical thinking:* Students are provided with models of critical thought that are incorporated into classroom activities, questions, and assignments.
- *Creative thinking:* Students are provided with models of creative thinking that develop skills that support innovative thinking and problem posing and solving.

- *Problem solving:* Students are engaged in real-world problem solving in each unit of study and learn the processes involved in such work.
- *Technology literacy:* Students use technology in multiple forms and formats as a tool in solving problems and to create generative products.
- *Information media literacy:* Students use multimedia to express ideas, research results, explore real-world problems, and evaluate information presented in media (graphs and diagrams) for mathematical accuracy.
- *Social skills:* Students work in small groups and develop the tools of collaborating, communicating, and working effectively with others on a common set of tasks.

Research Support for the Effort

Evidence-based practices that inform the teacher preparation and programming standards in gifted education relate to assessment, curriculum, instruction, and grouping issues, all of which are embedded within the Common Core State Standards and the NAGC-CEC (2006) Teacher Knowledge and Skill Standards for Gifted and Talented Education. These practices have an extensive research base (see *NAGC Research Base to Support the NAGC-CEC Teacher Preparation Standards in Gifted Education* [NAGC, 2006]).

The developers of the CCSS used national and international research on teaching and learning mathematics in the creation of the standards. In June 2010, the National Council of Teachers of Mathematics (NCTM), the National Council of Supervisors of Mathematics (NCSM), the Association of State Supervisors of Mathematics (ASSM), and the Association of Mathematics Teacher Educators (AMTE) issued a joint statement in support of the CCSS. As part of this support, they noted, "Finally, we strongly encourage and support both research about the standards themselves (e.g., research on specific learning trajectories and grade placement of specific content) and their implementation, as well as periodic review and revision based on such research" (p. 2). (See the joint statement at http://www.nctm.org/standards/content.aspx?id=26088.) In November 2011, the joint task force on the CCSS of these four organizations announced *A Priority Research Agenda for Understanding the Influence of the Common Core State Standards for Mathematics* (Heck, Weiss, & Pasley, 2011), which focused on the development of assessments, how assessments influence content and practices standards, the development and revision of curriculum materials, and state and district responses, as well as teacher responses, to the math standards. (See the recommendations and results from this research at http://www.mathedleadership.org.)

Also in November 2011, the Board of Directors of the National Council of Supervisors of Mathematics approved a position statement on *Improving Student Achievement by Expanding Opportunities for Our Most Promising Students of Mathematics* quoting NCTM and noting, "Without properly motivating, encouraging, and intellectually challenging gifted students, we may lose some of their mathematical talents forever" (p. 1). The introduction also quotes the National Science Board, which stated, "The U.S. education system too frequently fails to identify and develop our most talented and motivated students who will become the next generation of innovators" (NCSM, 2011, p. 5). Given this background, it is critical that these most promising "special needs students deserve a learning environment that lifts the ceiling, fuels their creativity and passion, and pushes them to make continuous progress throughout their academic careers" (NCSM, 2011, p. 1).

In 1980, the National Council of Teachers of Mathematics noted, "The student most neglected, in terms of realizing full potential, is the gifted student of mathematics. Outstanding mathematical ability is a precious societal resource, sorely needed to maintain leadership in a technological world" (p. 18). Two decades later, as the world became increasingly technological, the NCTM Task Force on the Mathematically Promising defined mathematical promise as a function of ability, motivation, belief, and experience or opportunity, stating that these are variables that can and should be maximized (Sheffield, Bennett, Berriozabal, DeArmond, & Wertheimer, 1999).

High-achieving students who experienced curricula that nurtured and developed mathematical enjoyment, passion, and talent had significantly higher achievement gains than a comparison group of students who had not had access to such programs (Gavin, Casa, Adelson, Carroll, & Sheffield, 2009). This type of curriculum is reflected in Figure 1, which depicts the importance of the development of positive student attitudes as well as mathematical sense-making, problem solving, and creativity. To create the mathematical innovators of tomorrow, educators need to help students develop mathematical passion, perseverance, and creativity in the face of difficult problems, and not just mathematical competence in computation and problem solving. Note that although making sense of mathematics and solving problems are critical, these abilities are not enough. Higher expectations are needed that include mathematical creativity where students are encouraged to create their own methods for making sense of and solving problems and raising new questions that are suggested during the solution of the original problem.

Several researchers have noted the importance of developing student enjoyment, interest, passion, and creativity when learning mathematics and not just skill with computation and algorithms. Many mention the importance of extracurricular activities, such as math circles and clubs, competitions, online games and activities, challenging puzzles and problems, research opportunities, mentors, and Saturday, afterschool, or summer math programs where students can build their passion for learning mathematics as they interact with others with similar interests and abilities. They also have cautioned that extracurricular activities should not be a substitute for engaging, challenging, and appropriately accelerated mathematics as part of the general education curricula (Barnett & Durden, 1993; Brody, 2004; Colangelo, Assouline, & Gross, 2004; Karp, 2010; Krutetskii,

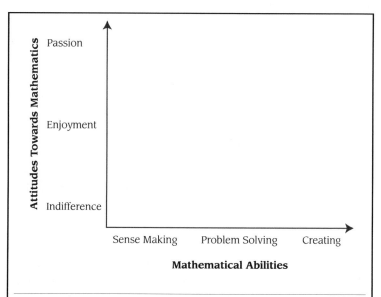

Figure 1. The intersection of attitudes with mathematical abilities. From "Using Curriculum to Develop Mathematical Promise in the Middle Grades," by M. K. Gavin and L. J. Sheffield, in *The Peak in the Middle: Developing Mathematically Gifted Students in the Middle Grades* (p. 54), by M. Saul, S. Assouline, and L. J. Sheffield (Eds.), 2010, Reston, VA: National Council of Teachers of Mathematics. Copyright 2010 by the National Council of Teachers of Mathematics. Reprinted with permission from the National Council of Teachers of Mathematics. All rights reserved.

1968/1976; Rothery, 2008; Rusczyk, 2012; Subotnik, Edmiston, & Rayhack, 2007; Warshauer et al., 2010).

One positive outcome of recent education reforms seems to be the increase in the numbers of high school students successfully passing Advanced Placement (AP) exams in calculus. As these numbers have increased, more students now receive credit for first-year calculus in high school than in college. Researchers caution that in spite of this increase, the numbers of students successfully completing the second or third course in calculus have declined, as have the numbers and percent of students who intend to major in engineering at the university level (Bressoud, 2009). Simple acceleration to increase AP Calculus numbers in high school seems to have had the unintended consequence of students either not desiring or not being successful in more advanced mathematics courses when they reach the university level. Because of this development, the Mathematical Association of America (MAA) and the National Council of Teachers of Mathematics (2012) have recommended that it is important to establish a mathematical foundation that will enable students to pursue whatever course of study interests them when they get to college. They suggested that faculty in colleges and secondary schools need to work together to strengthen the curriculum and the instruction so that advanced students who want to pursue mathematically intensive careers acquire the prerequisite mathematical knowledge. For example, calculus is a prerequisite for STEM fields at the university level, whereas statistics is more likely to be a prerequisite for the social sciences and business. If students are interested in STEM fields, they must be aware that they will need to take calculus in high school to be on track for more advanced courses at the university level. When students with potential in mathematics participate in accelerated classes that are taught by experienced teachers who are aware of their needs, they are more likely to take rigorous college courses, complete advanced degrees, and feel academically challenged and socially accepted (Colangelo et al., 2004; Gross, 2006; Kolitch & Brody, 1992; Swiatek, 1993).

Differentiating the Common Core State Standards for Gifted and Advanced Students

All differentiation is based on an understanding of the characteristics of gifted and high-potential students *and* the content standards within a domain. The new Common Core State Standards provide an opportunity for the field of gifted education to examine its practices and align them more fully to the 2010 NAGC Pre-K–Grade 12 Gifted Programming Standards for curriculum, instruction, and assessment. For example, similar to the NAGC Gifted Programming Standards, the CCSS emphasize problem solving (see Evidence-Based Practices 3.4.1–3.4.4, NAGC, 2010, p. 10, and Standards for Mathematical Practice 1, NGA & CCSSO, 2010a, p. 6). Because the Gifted Programming Standards in curriculum require educators to engage in two major tasks in curriculum planning—alignment to standards in the content areas and the development of a scope and sequence—using the CCSS is a natural point of departure. The effort must occur in vertical planning teams within districts and states in order to increase the likelihood of consistency and coherence in the process. There are three major strategies that may be employed to accomplish the task for gifted education:

- *Provide pathways with appropriate pacing of the CCSS for gifted learners.* Some of the CCSS address higher level skills and concepts that should receive focus throughout the years of schooling, such as a major emphasis on reasoning and sense-making. However, there are also discrete skills that may be clustered across grade levels and compressed around higher level skills and concepts for more efficient mastery by gifted students. Teachers might use preassessments in determining which students require more accelerated pacing. For example, within the CCSS domain of Measurement and Data, some students in first grade might be estimating lengths in standard units, while others might be solving problems involving measurement and estimation of liquid, volumes, and/or masses of objects (grade 3) or converting like measurement units within a given measurement system (grade 5).
- *Provide examples of differentiated task demands to address specific standards.* Standards like problem solving in mathematics lend themselves to differentiated interpretation through demonstrating what a typical learner on grade level might be able to do at a given stage of development versus what a gifted learner might be able to do. The differentiated examples should show greater complexity and creativity using a more advanced curriculum base. In mathematics, whereas typical learners might solve multistep word problems using a variety of models and strategies throughout grades K–12, gifted learners might pose and solve new, related problems of their own at an earlier stage of development. Other degrees of differentiation may take place by adding complexity to the task and using enrichment techniques that address student needs and district demographics, such as using mathematical equations and modeling to solve community problems.
- *Create interdisciplinary product demands to elevate learning for gifted students and to efficiently address multiple standards at once.* Because English language arts and mathematics

standards can be grouped together in application, much of the project work that gifted educators might already use could be revised to connect to the new CCSS and to show how multiple standards could be addressed across content areas. For example, research projects could be designed that address the research standard in English language arts and the data representation standard in mathematics by (a) delineating a product demand for research on an issue, (b) asking researchable questions that require quantitative approaches, (c) using multiple sources to answer them, (d) collecting data, (e) interpreting data (e.g., by creating a scatterplot and deciding if there is a line of best fit and describing the related variables), and then (f) representing findings in tables, graphs, and other visual displays that are explained in text and presented to an audience with implications for a plan of action. Such a project might be possible for the gifted learner at an earlier grade than for a typical learner.

To differentiate the Common Core State Standards for Mathematics, educators need to be aware of the eight Standards for Mathematical Practice and additional standards that should be considered for promising mathematics students before differentiating the curriculum. This section will address these needs and provide specific examples of differentiation that examine learning progressions in operations and algebraic thinking, fractions and the number system, geometry, and statistics and probability.

The Common Core State Standards for Mathematical Practice

When considering the implications of the CCSS for the development of mathematical talent, it is important to take into account the eight Standards for Mathematical Practice that educators should seek to develop in their students in addition to the individual mathematics content standards. These Standards for Mathematical Practice are an integral part of the Common Core State Standards for Mathematics and are described in detail (NGA & CCSSO, 2010a, pp. 6–8). These build on the NCTM (2000) process standards of problem solving, reasoning and proof, communication, representation, and connections, and include the strands of mathematical proficiency specified in the National Research Council's report *Adding It Up* (Kilpatrick, Swafford, & Findell, 2001): adaptive reasoning, strategic competence, conceptual understanding (comprehension of mathematical concepts, operations, and relations), procedural fluency (skill in carrying out procedures flexibly, accurately, efficiently, and appropriately), and productive disposition (habitual inclination to see mathematics as sensible, useful, and worthwhile, coupled with a belief in diligence and one's own efficacy). The eight Standards for Mathematical Practice for all students from kindergarten through college and careers are:

1. Make sense of problems and persevere in solving them.
2. Reason abstractly and quantitatively.
3. Construct viable arguments and critique the reasoning of others.
4. Model with mathematics.
5. Use appropriate tools strategically.
6. Attend to precision.
7. Look for and make use of structure.
8. Look for and express regularity in repeated reasoning.

It is important that students actively engage in these practices daily in their mathematics classes. Students need ongoing opportunities to experience the joy of investigating rich concepts in depth and applying mathematical reasoning and justification to a variety of scientific, engineering, and other problems.

In order to support mathematically advanced students and to develop students who have the expertise, perseverance, creativity, and willingness to take risks and recover from failure, which is necessary for them to become mathematics innovators, we propose that a ninth Standard for Mathematical Practice be added for the development of promising mathematics students—a standard on mathematical creativity and innovation: *Solve problems in novel ways and pose new mathematical questions of interest to investigate.*

The characteristics of the new proposed standard would be that students are encouraged and supported in taking risks, embracing challenge, solving problems in a variety of ways, posing new mathematical questions of interest to investigate, and being passionate about mathematical investigations.

Developing Innovative and Creative Mathematicians

To aid in the development of passionate, innovative, and creative mathematicians, teachers might use a heuristic such as the one shown in Figure 2. Using this heuristic, students may start at any point on the diagram and proceed in any order. One possible order might be:

- Relate the problem to other problems that you have solved. How is this similar to other mathematical ideas that you have seen? How is it different?
- Investigate the problem. Think deeply and ask questions.
- Evaluate your findings. Did you answer the question? Does the answer make sense?
- Communicate your results. How can you best let others know what you have discovered?
- Create new questions to explore. What else would you like to find out about this topic? Start a new investigation.

To assist students in their creation of new mathematical insights, some suggested questions for creative mathematical investigations include the following (Sheffield, 2006):

- *Who?* Who has another solution? Who has another method? Who agrees or disagrees?
- *What or what if?* What patterns do I see in these data? What generalizations might I make from the patterns? What proof do I have? What are the chances? What is

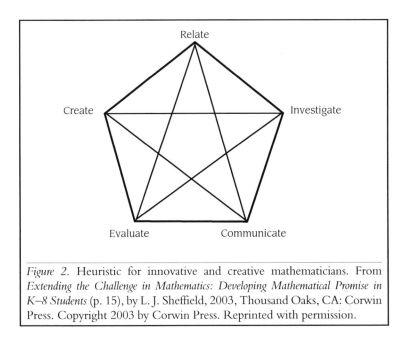

Figure 2. Heuristic for innovative and creative mathematicians. From *Extending the Challenge in Mathematics: Developing Mathematical Promise in K–8 Students* (p. 15), by L. J. Sheffield, 2003, Thousand Oaks, CA: Corwin Press. Copyright 2003 by Corwin Press. Reprinted with permission.

the best answer, best method of solution, or best strategy to begin with? What if I change one or more parts of the problem? What new problems might I create?

- *When?* When does this work? When does this not work?
- *Where?* Where did that come from? Where should I start? Where might I go next? Where might I find additional information?
- *Why or why not?* Why does that work? If it does not work, why does it not work?
- *How?* How is this like other mathematical problems or patterns that I have seen? How does it differ? How does this relate to real-life situations or models? How many solutions are possible? How many ways might I to represent, simulate, model, or visualize these ideas? How many ways might I sort, organize, and present this information?

Even our best mathematics students are often not encouraged to be creative. Educators need to support them as they move from questions with one right answer to those that require reasoning and justification and to problems and explorations that have several solutions or related problems that will deepen and extend the concepts being learned. Educators need to remember that the real learning frequently begins after the original problem has been solved.

If educators wish for students to develop a deeper understanding of concepts and to become creative and investigative mathematicians, they should use criteria for assessment that encourage depth and creativity, such as those noted by Sheffield (2000):

- *Depth of understanding:* the extent to which core concepts are understood, explored, and developed.
- *Fluency:* the number of different correct answers, methods of solution, or new questions formulated.
- *Flexibility:* the number of different categories of answers, methods, or questions.
- *Originality:* solutions, methods, or questions that are unique and show insight.
- *Elaboration or elegance:* clarity and quality of expression of thinking, including charts, graphs, drawings, models, and words.
- *Generalizations:* patterns that are noted, hypothesized, and verified for larger categories.
- *Extensions:* related questions that are asked and explored, especially those involving why and what if.

The instructional pace is also a critical consideration in the education of gifted students in mathematics. Advanced learners may demonstrate rapid or early mastery of some of the mathematics standards, especially those involving skill at computation and mastery of algorithms, requiring accelerative opportunities at key stages of development. Appropriate pacing for these students, including accelerated courses, means that students have the time and opportunity to delve deeply and creatively into topics, projects, and problems of interest. Therefore, it's important that advanced learners receive their instruction from well-prepared teachers who are knowledgeable regarding mathematics and strategies to use with advanced learners.

Teachers of the gifted should be mindful of the importance of providing problem-finding and problem-solving skills and strategies to stimulate mathematical and spatial reasoning and to work with a wide range of mathematical topics, such as number theory, geometry, and discrete mathematics. Early exposure to topics such as probability, statistics, and logic also are viable approaches to be used to support applied and cross-curricular skills, including conducting meaningful research in science and engineering. Extracurricular opportunities such as math clubs, circles, competitions, mentors, and online experiences should also be readily available without additional cost to students.

In encouraging these high levels of mathematical creativity and giftedness (Chapin, O'Connor, & Anderson, 2009), teachers should realize that the role of students is to:

- think, reason, make sense, and go deeper;
- talk to a partner and generate new ideas;
- repeat and rephrase what others have said and explain why they agree or disagree;
- make generalizations and justify conclusions;
- add on new ideas, new methods of solution, new questions, and original problems and related solutions;
- record solutions, reasoning, and questions;
- pose new mathematical questions of interest to investigate; and
- create innovative mathematical problems and solutions.

The role of the teacher is to:

- ask questions that encourage mathematical creativity, reasoning, and sense-making;
- elicit, engage, and challenge each student's thinking;
- listen carefully to students' ideas;

- ask students to clarify, justify, connect, and extend their ideas;
- assist students in attaching mathematical notation and language to their ideas;
- reflect on student understanding, differentiate instruction, and encourage participation; and
- guide students to resources, including those online, in print, and in person, such as mentors, apprenticeships, competitions, clubs, math circles, and other extracurricular opportunities.

Specific Examples for Differentiating Mathematics

The Standards for Mathematical Content appear in a variety of domains depending on the grade level. These are:
- Counting and Cardinality (K)
- Operations and Algebraic Thinking (K–5)
- Number and Operations in Base Ten (K–5)
- Measurement and Data (K–5)
- Geometry (K–HS)
- Number and Operations–Fractions (3–5)
- Ratios and Proportional Relationships (6–7)
- The Number System (6–8)
- Expressions and Equations (6–8)
- Statistics and Probability (6–HS)
- Functions (8–HS)
- Number and Quantity (HS)
- Algebra (HS)
- Modeling (HS)

The following pages offer examples of activities that use the eight Standards for Mathematical Practice and support the implementation of the Common Core State Standards for Mathematics. The advanced activities also make use of the proposed ninth Standard for Mathematical Practice on mathematical creativity and innovation. (Options for mathematical creativity are italicized.)

The sample activities were designed to give exemplars in a variety of areas including number and operations, algebraic thinking, geometry, and data and statistics. Sample activities are given for primary, intermediate, middle, and high school standards. Each activity begins with a selected task, gives a variety of questions for both typical and advanced learners, and describes suggestions for implementation that include ideas for different types of formative and summative assessment. Note that sometimes the initial problem is the same for both typical and advanced learners, and questions and formative assessments are used to differentiate and develop mathematical creativity and giftedness.

Formative assessment in these activities includes the use of pretests, differentiation of tasks and questions to assess during the problem-solving process, observation and analysis of student work, portfolios, and authentic cross-disciplinary tasks and research.

Sample Activities Aligned With the Common Core State Standards for Mathematics

Subject: Math Learning Progressions: Patterns

Domains: Operations and Algebraic Thinking (Grades 3 and 5); Functions (Grade 8 and High School)

Grade 3
Domain: Operations and Algebraic Thinking

Pattern A:

Front

Row 1:	1	2	3	4	5	6	7	8	9	10
Row 2:	11	12	13	14	15	16	17	18	19	20
Row 3:	21	22	23	24	25	26	27	28	29	30

The first three rows of Cedar Creek Elementary School's gym are in this pattern. The rest of the seats follow the same pattern.

Pattern B:

Front

Row 1:	1	2	3	4	5	6
Row 2:	7	8	9	10	11	12
Row 3:	13	14	15	16	17	18

The first three rows of Ridgewood Elementary School's gym are in this pattern. The rest of the seats follow the same pattern.

Grade 3, *continued*

	Typical Learner	Advanced Learner
Standard: 3.OA.9. Identify arithmetic patterns (including patterns in the addition table or multiplication table), and explain them using properties of operations.	Have students use Pattern B to answer the prompts below: 1. Deedra is in Seat 36. What row is she in? 2. Tom is two rows behind and two seats to the right of Seat 52. What is his seat number? 3. Rondell is in Row 7. What is the largest number of the seat that he might be sitting in? Explain how you found Rondell's seat number. 4. Give a rule for finding the largest seat number in any row using S to stand for the seat number and R to stand for the number of the row. Explain your reasoning.	Have students use both Patterns A and B to answer the prompts below: 1. I am in the third seat from the left in a secret row. For each pattern, give a rule for finding my seat number, using S to stand for the seat number and R to stand for the number of the secret row. 2. Compare Patterns A and B. What is alike and what is different? Is one set more difficult than the other? Why or why not? Compare the method you used to answer the questions with someone else in your class. Did you use the same method? Did you get the same answer? 3. *Make up your own seating problems and trade with a friend to solve them. Do you both get the same answer? Did you use the same method?*
Implementation	The teacher uses the first three typical learner questions for Pattern B with all of the students in a group discussion. Each student shares his or her responses individually, perhaps using white boards or clicker responses on a computer system. These responses are used as a formative assessment to determine if students need to respond to the final typical learner question on their own for Pattern B or move to advanced learner questions. The teacher allows advanced learners to work on the more complex questions related to Patterns A and B independently, in small groups, or in pairs. The general education learners then work on the four typical learner questions for Pattern A with the teacher. The teacher meets with the advanced learners to discuss their answers to the questions they answered individually. *The teacher might want to have the advanced learners share their created seating problems with the whole class.*	

Grade 5
Domain: Operations and Algebraic Thinking

Pattern C:
Front

Row 1:	1			
Row 2:	2	3		
Row 3:	4	5	6	
Row 4:	7	8	9	10

The first four rows of Castleman Creek Middle School's gym are in this pattern. The rest of the seats follow the same pattern.

Pattern D:
Front

Row 1:	1	2						
Row 2:	3	4	5	6				
Row 3:	7	8	9	10	11	12		
Row 4:	13	14	15	16	17	18	19	20

The first four rows of Woodway Middle School's gym are in this pattern. The rest of the seats follow the same pattern.

Standard	Typical Learner	Advanced Learner
Standard 5.OA.3. Generate two numerical patterns using two given rules. Identify apparent relationships between corresponding terms. Form ordered pairs consisting of corresponding terms from the two patterns, and graph the ordered pairs on a coordinate plane.	Have students use Pattern C to answer the prompts below: 1. Will is in Seat 15. What row is he in? 2. Maureen is directly behind Seat 42. What is her seat number? 3. I am in the last seat on the right in a secret row. You can find my seat number by multiplying the row number by one more than the row number and then dividing the answer by two. Write an equation *continued*	Have students use Pattern C to answer the first three prompts below: 1. I am in the last seat on the right in a secret row. Give a rule for finding my seat number using S to stand for the seat number and R to stand for the number of the secret row. 2. Complete the following chart for Pattern C using your rule: *continued*

continued

Grade 5, continued

for finding my seat number, using S to stand for the seat number and R to stand for the number of the secret row.

4. Complete the following chart using your rule:

Row Number	Last Seat Number
1	1
2	3
3	6
4	10
5	
6	
7	
8	
n	

5. Graph the ordered pairs for the last seat in each row on a coordinate plane using the row number as the x-coordinate and the seat number as the y-coordinate.

6. Create a chart of the ordered pairs for the seat with the largest number in each row for the seats in Pattern D. Graph this on a coordinate plane. Compare this to your graph from Question 5. List two things that are different, and explain the differences.

Row Number	Last Seat Number
1	1
2	3
3	6
4	10
5	
6	
7	
8	
n	

3. Graph the ordered pairs for the last seat in each row on a coordinate plane using the row number as the x-coordinate and the seat number as the y-coordinate.

4. Answer Questions 1–3 using Pattern D. What is alike and what is different? Is one set harder than the other? Why or why not? Compare the method you used to answer the questions with someone else in your class. Did you use the same method? Did you get the same answer?

5. Make up your own seating problems and trade with a friend to solve them. Do you both get the same answer? Did you use the same method?

Students who want to delve more deeply into these patterns should be encouraged to research triangular numbers. For very interested students, suggest research into other figurate numbers.

Grade 5, *continued*	
Implementation	The teacher uses the first two typical learner questions for Pattern C with all of the students in a group discussion. Each student shares his or her responses individually. These responses are used as a formative assessment to determine if the student needs to respond to the rest of the typical learner questions or move to advanced learner questions. The teacher allows advanced learners to work on the more complex questions independently, in small groups, or in pairs. The general education learners work on typical learner Questions 3–4 with the teacher and Questions 5–6 independently. The teacher then meets with the advanced learners to discuss their answers to the questions. *The teacher might want to have the advanced learners share their created seating problems with the whole class.*
Grade 8 and High School **Domain: Functions**	Pattern E: Front Row 1: 1 Row 2: 3 5 Row 3: 7 9 11 Row 4: 13 15 17 19 Row 5: 21 23 25 27 29 The first five rows of Woodgate High School's gym are in this pattern. The rest of the seats follow the same pattern. Pattern F: Front Row 1: 2 Row 2: 4 6 Row 3: 8 10 12 Row 4: 14 16 18 20 Row 5: 22 24 26 28 30 The first five rows of Taylor High School's gym are in this pattern. The rest of the seats follow the same pattern.

Grade 8 and High School, *continued*

	Typical Learner	Advanced Learner
Standard 8.F.5. Describe qualitatively the functional relationship between two quantities by analyzing a graph (e.g., where the function is increasing or decreasing, linear or nonlinear). **Standard F.BF.2. Write arithmetic and geometric sequences both recursively and with an explicit formula, use them to model situations, and translate between the two forms.**	Have students use Pattern E to answer the prompts below: 1. Jose is in Seat 65. What row is he in? 2. Louise is in Seat 121. What row is she in? 3. I am in the middle seat in a secret row. Give a rule for finding my seat number, using S to stand for the seat number and R to stand for the number of the secret row. (Hint: Make a table with the row number in the first column and the matching seat number for the middle seat in the second column. Graph the ordered pairs. Look for patterns. Is this a linear or a nonlinear function?)	Have students use Pattern E to answer the first two prompts below: 1. I am in the last seat in a secret row. Give a rule for finding my seat number, using S to stand for the seat number and R to stand for the number of the secret row. 2. Will the graph of your rule be a linear or nonlinear function? Explain how you know. To check, graph the ordered pairs using the row number for the x-coordinate and the number of the last seat in the row for the y-coordinate. 3. Answer Questions 1–2 for Pattern F. 4. Compare your responses for Patterns E and F. What is alike and what is different? Is one set harder than the other? Why or why not? Compare the method you used to answer the questions with someone else in your class. Did you use the same method? Did you get the same answer? 5. *Make up your own seating problems and trade with a friend to solve them. Did you both get the same answer? Did you use the same methods?*
Implementation	The teacher uses the first three typical learner questions for Pattern E with all of the students in a group discussion. Each student shares his or her responses individually. These responses are used as a formative assessment to determine if the student needs the hints for Question 3. The teacher allows advanced learners to work on the more complex questions independently, in small groups, or in pairs. The general education learners are given the hints and work with the teacher to complete the typical learner questions. They then complete the same typical learner questions for Pattern F independently. The teacher meets with the advanced learners to discuss their answers to the questions. *The teacher might want to have the advanced learners share their created seating problems with the whole class.*	

Note. Problems for Math Learning Progressions: Patterns are adapted from Sheffield (2003).

Subject: Math Learning Progression: Fractions
Domain: Number and Operations–Fractions (Grades 3–5); The Number System (Grade 7)

Grade 3 Domain: Number and Operations–Fractions	Typical Learner	Advanced Learner
Standard 3.NF.2b. Understand a fraction as a number on the number line; represent fractions on a number line diagram. Represent a fraction a/b on a number line diagram by marking off a lengths $1/b$ from 0. Recognize that the resulting interval has size a/b and that its endpoint locates the number a/b on the number line.	1. Give students the following fractions: $$\frac{1}{2}, \frac{1}{3}, \frac{1}{4}, \frac{2}{3}, \frac{3}{4}, \frac{4}{4}, \frac{2}{6}, \frac{3}{6}, \frac{5}{6}, \frac{6}{6}$$ 2. Have students locate each of the fractions on a number line. 3. Ask students to list two pairs of equivalent fractions and explain their reasoning. 4. Have students list all of the fractions in order from the least to the greatest.	1. *Have students create a fraction by choosing a whole number between 1 and 50 for the numerator and a whole number between 2 and 98 for the denominator.* 2. *Have students estimate where their fraction belongs on the number line and give a reason for the choice.* 3. *Have students get together in groups of 6–8 and order their fractions from least to greatest.* 4. *Have students justify their order using different concrete models and abstract strategies such as common numerators, benchmarks, and common denominators.*
Implementation	Give students a pretest on fractions that includes locating fractions on a number line, finding equivalent fractions, ordering fractions, and using fractions with denominators of halves, thirds, fourths, and sixths. Student responses are used as a formative assessment to determine if the student needs to complete the typical or advanced activity. As a result of the pretest, typical learners will work on ordering halves, thirds, fourths, and sixths on a number line with the teacher and then with more complex problems independently. Students who have mastered these concepts should work independently, in pairs, or in small groups together on the advanced problem while the others work with the teacher on the typical learner questions. After working with the typical learners, the teacher should give them another group of fractions to order while she listens to the advanced students explain their reasoning for ordering fractions such as $\frac{18}{35}$ and $\frac{29}{60}$. For a pair of fractions such as this, students should be able to use benchmarks to explain why $\frac{18}{35}$ is slightly more than $\frac{1}{2}$ and $\frac{29}{60}$ is slightly less than $\frac{1}{2}$, therefore understanding that $\frac{29}{60}$ is less than $\frac{18}{35}$. *The teacher might want to have the advanced learners share their created fractions and discuss their concrete models and abstract strategies.*	

Grade 5
Domain: Number and Operations–Fractions

	Typical Learner	Advanced Learner
Standard 5.NF.1. Use equivalent fractions as a strategy to add and subtract fractions. Add and subtract fractions with unlike denominators (including mixed numbers) by replacing given fractions with equivalent fractions in such a way as to produce an equivalent sum or difference of fractions with like denominators.	1. Given sets of two fractions to add or subtract, students will complete the operation by replacing the given fractions with equivalent fractions. For example, $\frac{2}{3} + \frac{5}{4} = \frac{8}{12} + \frac{15}{12} = \frac{23}{12}$. In general, $\frac{a}{b} + \frac{c}{d} = \frac{(ad+bc)}{bd}$.	1. Given $\frac{a}{b} + \frac{c}{d} = 1$, students will write as many equations as possible substituting whole numbers 1–9 for $a, b, c,$ and d. 2. Repeat this for $\frac{a}{b} - \frac{c}{d} = 1$. 3. *Encourage students to create their own fraction puzzles for each other. Students who have mastered addition and subtraction of fractions might want to use all four operations in their puzzles.*
Implementation	Give students a pretest on fractions that includes adding and subtracting fractions and mixed numbers with unlike denominators. Students who have mastered these concepts should work individually, in pairs, or in small groups on the advanced problems while the others work with the teacher on the typical learner question. After working with the typical learners, the teacher should give them another group of fractions and mixed numbers to add and subtract, perhaps including the advanced questions, while she listens to the advanced students explain their reasoning. *Advanced students may share the puzzles they have created with the others.*	

Grade 7
Domain: The Number System

	Typical Learner	Advanced Learner
Standard 7.NS.1d. Apply and extend previous understandings of operations with fractions to add, subtract, multiply, and divide rational numbers. Apply and extend previous understandings of addition and subtraction to add and subtract rational numbers; represent addition and subtraction on a horizontal or vertical number line diagram. Apply properties of operations as strategies to add and subtract rational numbers.	1. Given sets of two rational numbers to add or subtract (e.g., $-3\frac{2}{5}+1\frac{3}{4}$), students will complete the operation and show their reasoning on a number line. 2. Given sets of two rational numbers to multiply or divide (e.g., $3\frac{2}{5}\cdot 1\frac{3}{4}$), students will complete the operation and explain their reasoning with words, equations, or diagrams such as arrays. For example, have students draw pictures of the problem. As an example, have students draw a picture in which they describe dividing $\frac{5}{8}$ by $\frac{2}{5}$.	1. Given $\frac{a}{b}+\frac{c}{d}=-1$, students will write as many equations as possible substituting the integers -9 through $+9$ for the variables. 2. Repeat this using puzzles such as: • $A\frac{b}{c}+D\frac{e}{f}=1$ • $\frac{a}{b}-\frac{c}{d}=1$ • $A\frac{b}{c}\cdot\frac{d}{e}=1$ • $A\frac{b}{c}+\frac{d}{e}=-1$ 3. *Encourage students to create their own fraction puzzles for each other using a combination of operations.*
Implementation	Give students a pretest on fractions that includes multiplying and dividing positive and negative fractions and mixed numbers. Students who have mastered these concepts should work individually, in pairs, or in small groups on the advanced problems while the others work with the teacher on the typical learner questions. After working with the typical learners, the teacher should give them another group of fractions and mixed numbers to multiply and divide, perhaps including the advanced puzzles, while she listens to the advanced students explain their reasoning. *Advanced students may share the puzzles they have created with the others.*	

Note. Problems for Math Learning Progressions: Fractions are adapted from Gavin, Sheffield, Dailey, and Chapin (2008) and Sheffield, Chapin, and Gavin (2010a).

Subject: Math Learning Progressions
Domain: Geometry (Grades 3, 5, and 8)

Grade 3 Domain: Geometry	Cut out two identical squares. Leave one square whole, and cut the other square along the diagonal.	
	Typical Learner	**Advanced Learner**
Standard: 3.G.1. Understand that shapes in different categories (e.g., rhombuses, rectangles, and others) may share attributes (e.g., having four sides), and that the shared attributes can define a larger category (e.g., quadrilaterals). Recognize rhombuses, rectangles, and squares as examples of quadrilaterals, and draw examples of quadrilaterals that do not belong to any of these subcategories.	1. Using two or more of their shapes, have students combine them to make rhombuses, rectangles, squares, and other quadrilaterals. Students should trace and label each shape. 2. Have students describe the characteristics of each of these shapes.	1. Using two or more of their shapes, have students combine them to make as many different polygons as possible. Students should trace and label each shape. 2. Have students sort their polygons into categories and describe the attributes that define each category. 3. Have students sort their polygons into different categories and describe the attributes that define each category. 4. *Ask students how many different classification schemes they can create. Students should compare their responses with a partner. Have students discuss how mathematicians might have used similar categories to define types of quadrilaterals such as squares, rectangles, and rhombuses.*
Implementation	Students who are good at computation are often not the same students who excel at spatial visualization. Spatial visualization is critical to several types of careers, including engineering, architecture, and surgery, and should be developed throughout K–12. Observe students as they create different shapes and ask them to describe the characteristics of the shapes they are creating. Use an observation checklist to keep track of student progress. Give students increasingly difficult challenges as they work individually or with a partner who is at a similar level.	

Grade 5 Domain: Geometry	Use a seven-piece tangram set for this activity.	
	Typical Learner	**Advanced Learner**
5.G.3. Understand that attributes belonging to a category of two-dimensional figures also belong to all subcategories of that category. For example, all rectangles have four right angles and squares are rectangles, so all squares have four right angles. 5.G.4. Classify two-dimensional figures in a hierarchy based on properties.	1. Using two or more of the tangram pieces, students should combine them to make a variety of polygons. Have students trace and label each shape. 2. Have students place all of the quadrilaterals in one pile and place all of the nonquadrilaterals in another pile. Ask students where they placed the parallelograms. Why did they place them there? 3. Have students sort all of the quadrilaterals into parallelograms and nonparallelograms. Ask students where they placed the rectangles. Why did they place them there? 4. Have students sort all of the parallelograms into rectangles and nonrectangles. Ask students where they placed the squares. Why did they place them there?	1. Using two or more of the tangram pieces, have students combine them to make a variety of polygons. Have students trace each shape onto a different 3" x 5" index card. 2. Play "Shape Rummy." In this game, students start with a deck of cards, each card with a drawing of a different polygon. These should be cards that students have created using the tracings of their tans. These might include a variety of squares, nonsquare rectangles, rhombuses, other parallelograms, trapezoids, triangles, pentagons, and hexagons. Students play a game similar to Rummy where the cards are dealt out and students make sets of three cards. A set of three squares or a set of three trapezoids is worth 10 points, a set of three rectangles or a set of three rhombuses is worth 5 points, and a set of three parallelograms or three regular polygons is worth 3 points. 3. After playing the game, students should discuss the following items: • Why is a set of three squares worth more than a set of three rectangles (rhombuses)? (Because all squares are also rectangles [rhombuses], so there are always more rectangles [rhombuses] than squares.)

Grade 5, *continued*

	• How many points would you give for a set of three shapes with at least one right angle? Justify your answer. (They should give fewer than 5 points because all rectangles will have right angles, as will other shapes such as right triangles, so there will always be more shapes with right angles than there are rectangles.) • Make up another category of shapes and justify the number of points for that category.

Implementation

Observe students as they combine and sort shapes and ask them to describe the characteristics of the categories. Use an observation checklist to keep track of student progress, and check to make sure that they understand the hierarchy of the classification schemes. For example, make sure that they realize that all quadrilaterals are polygons, all parallelograms are quadrilaterals, all rectangles and rhombuses are parallelograms, and all squares are rectangles and rhombuses. Give students increasingly difficult challenges as they work individually or with a partner who is at a similar level. Once the hierarchy is understood, let students play the Shape Rummy game and answer the questions. For more challenge, sort the shapes into three-loop Venn diagrams.

Grade 8
Domain: Geometry

Draw any quadrilateral on a coordinate grid. List the coordinates of each of the four vertices.

	Typical Learner	Advanced Learner
Standard 8.G.3. Describe the effect of dilations, translations, rotations, and reflections on two-dimensional figures using coordinates.	Have students complete the activities below: 1. Draw a similar quadrilateral on the coordinate grid where each of the sides is twice the length of the first one. List the coordinates of each of these four vertices.	*Have students create a transformation puzzle following the steps below:* 1. *Using the quadrilateral already drawn, use at least three of the four transformations (dilations, translations, rotations, or reflections) to create a series of similar quadrilaterals. Record the steps and the coordinates of each quadrilateral.*

Grade 8, *continued*	
	2. Draw a quadrilateral congruent to the original on the coordinate grid that is translated 3 spaces to the right and 2 spaces down from the original. List the coordinates of each of these four vertices. 3. Draw a quadrilateral congruent to the original on the coordinate grid that is rotated 90 degrees to the left about the origin. List the coordinates of each of these four vertices. 4. Draw a quadrilateral congruent to the original on the coordinate grid that is reflected over the *x*-axis. List the coordinates of each of these four vertices.	2. *Give the coordinates of the original and final quadrilaterals to a partner. The partner must then determine a sequence of transformations that will result in the final quadrilateral. The partner compares these steps with the puzzle maker.* 3. *Partners should discuss if the steps are the same. Why or why not?*
Implementation	Use observation and student performance to assess students as they plot polygons on a coordinate plane. Ask them questions about the effect of dilations, translations, rotations, and reflections on two-dimensional figures using coordinates. Use an observation checklist to keep track of student progress. Give students increasingly difficult challenges as they work individually or with a partner who is at a similar level. *Encourage students to create and solve transformation puzzles with more than two steps as they become more proficient.*	

Note. Problems for Math Learning Progressions are adapted from Gavin et al. (2008), Sheffield (2003), and Sheffield et al. (2010b).

Subject: Math Learning Progression
Domains: Measurement and Data (Grade 3); Statistics and Probability (Grades 6, 8, and High School)

Grade 3 Domain: Measurement and Data	Ask students to choose a topic area in which they might make an impact using survey results (e.g., asking student preferences for adding a new healthy choice to the school cafeteria menu or choosing the best location for a field trip). Create questions, survey a large number of students, record, and compile the data.	
	Typical Learner	**Advanced Learner**
Standard: 3.MD.3. Represent and interpret data. Draw a scaled picture graph and a scaled bar graph to represent a data set with several categories. Solve one- and two-step "how many more" and "how many less" problems using information presented in scaled bar graphs. For example, draw a bar graph in which each square in the bar graph might represent 5 pets.	1. Students will draw a scaled bar graph and a scaled picture graph to display their results. 2. *Each student should create 3 one-step problems and 2 two-step problems that can be answered by looking at one of the graphs. Students will trade problems with a partner. After both have worked the problems, they will compare answers and reasoning.*	1. *Using the data collected, students will write a letter to a decision maker convincing that person to make a change based on their data. Students should use graphs and charts to support their arguments.*
Implementation	The class will work together to decide on an issue or issues and develop survey questions. All students should work in pairs to collect data. Students then should work individually or in pairs to create scaled bar or picture graphs to display the data collected and develop questions that can be answered using information from the graphs. These questions will give students a chance to work on different levels. *Students at a more advanced level can create a letter and make a presentation using the graphs to justify the requested changes. Student interest and self-assessment might be used to determine who is ready for the advanced level.*	

Grade 6 Domain: Statistics and Probability	Analyze class testing data. These might be data from a standardized test or from a recent math class quiz or test. Be sure all personal identifying data have been removed. Using the given data, have students complete the following activities.	
	Typical Learner	**Advanced Learner**
Standard: 6.SP.2. Develop understanding of statistical variability. Understand that a set of data collected to answer a statistical question has a distribution which can be described by its center, spread, and overall shape.	Have students complete the following: 1. Show the results on a line plot. 2. Make a stem and leaf plot of all of the scores. 3. Find the mean, median, mode, and range. When do we use each one? 4. Display the data in a box plot. 5. Describe how you might use the line plot and the box plot to describe the spread of the data. 6. How might you use the plots to determine whether the mean is greater or less than the median? How does this match your numerical results?	Have students complete the following: 1. Obtain testing data from two different tests. These might be the same test taken by two different classes of students or two different tests taken by the same students. Complete typical learner Steps 1–6. 2. Compare the line plot and box plots as well as several measures, including mean, median, mode, and range. Which class (or test) had the best results? Justify your conclusion. 4. *What suggestions do you have for next steps when planning future mathematics lessons based on your analysis of the testing results? Present your findings to the math teachers.*
Implementation	The class will work together to analyze and answer questions about testing data. These questions will give students a chance to work on different levels. Student interest and self-assessment might be used to determine who is ready for the advanced level. Students who choose to analyze testing data to suggest future lessons will hopefully have a vested interest in improving their own learning of mathematics as well as that of the entire class.	
Grade 8 and High School Domain: Statistics and Probability	Students will collect data on the battery life of cell phones. Ask students to use their phones as usual but not to charge them again until the batteries are completely dead. Each student should record the number of hours that the battery lasted from a full charge until the battery died. They should also record the number of minutes they were actively using the phone for voice or text messages or other active uses. Make a chart of the usage of the phone with the number of minutes they actively used the phone in the first column and the number of hours the battery lasted in the second column. Using the given data, have students complete the following activities.	

Grade 8 and High School, *continued*		
	Typical Learner	**Advanced Learner**
Standard 8.SP.1. Investigate patterns of association in bivariate data. Construct and interpret scatter plots for bivariate measurement data to investigate patterns of association between two quantities. Describe patterns such as clustering, outliers, positive or negative association, linear association, and nonlinear association. **Standard S-IC.6. Make inferences and justify conclusions from sample surveys, experiments, and observational studies. Evaluate reports based on data.**	Have students complete the following: 1. Name the independent and dependent variables. Make a scatter plot of the data. 2. Describe patterns such as clustering, outliers, positive or negative association, linear association, and nonlinear association. 3. Draw a line of best fit. Explain how you chose this line. Find the slope and y-intercept. Write an equation for your line of best fit and describe your method. 4. Locate research reports on a topic of interest that make use of scatter plots and lines of best fit. Analyze the data and the reported outcomes. Write a critique of the reports.	Have students complete the following: 1. Design an experiment to determine whether batteries on some phones last longer than others. 2. Display data from your experiment using a scatter plot for each type of battery. Write an equation for the line of best fit for each. What does this tell you about your two variables? 3. Write a report evaluating the batteries. Include your scatter plots and your equations. Include how you used your line of best fit to evaluate the batteries. 4. Choose another topic and design an experiment to test your hypothesis that makes use of scatter plots and lines of best fit. Create a mathematical model to explain your data.
Implementation	Student interest and self-assessment might be used to determine who is ready for the advanced level. Students without expertise in designing experiments and analyzing data using scatter plots and lines of best fit should be encouraged and supported as they master these concepts and construct their own experiments and research designs.	

Linking Mathematics and English Language Arts Standards

Because standards often can be addressed across subject areas rather than only in one domain, this booklet includes examples of how to consider linking the math standards and the English language arts standards. Other areas of learning that can be applied to standards-based tasks illustrate the efficiency and effectiveness that can be achieved through such compression and the differentiation for gifted learners that results.

There are two ways to remodel content to engage and motivate highly able learners by making cross-disciplinary connections. Although the strategies are related, they are distinct. The first approach is to use cross-disciplinary content. The second is to integrate standards from English language arts, mathematics, and other disciplines. Following are a few examples for each strategy.

Using Cross-Disciplinary Content

This strategy capitalizes on an area of interest in one discipline to engage learners in another. Begin with a standard from the CCSS for Mathematics or English Language Arts. Then draw in other content areas to give students opportunities to apply the standard. Examples are included below.

- *Mathematics Standard 3.OA.9. Identify arithmetic patterns (including patterns in the addition table or multiplication table), and explain them using properties of operations.* The idea in this standard is to identify and explain arithmetic patterns. Extend this idea beyond mathematics to motivate learners. Ask students to also identify and explain patterns in nature, in architecture, or in music. Use mathematics to describe and generalize the patterns observed.

- *Mathematics Standard 7.SP.4. Use measures of center and measures of variability for numerical data from random samples to draw informal comparative inferences about two populations.* Students can choose any content area to demonstrate mastery of this standard. For example, have students identify data that are likely to be false, erroneous, or otherwise highly questionable. Students might read that Organization X claims that 500,000 people per week experience a theft. Is that statement likely given the fact that there are 310,000,000 people in the U.S. and 500,000 times 52 weeks translates to 26,000,000? That would mean that approximately 1 in 12 people are affected each year. Data presented in media such as *USA Today* are useful for this type of activity.

Integrating Standards

This strategy combines standards from two or more disciplines to add complexity. Examples are included below.

- *Mathematics Standard 5.OA.3. Generate two numerical patterns using two given rules. Identify apparent relationships between corresponding terms; and English Language Arts Standard RF.5.3. Know and apply grade-level phonics and word analysis skills in decoding words. Use combined knowledge of all letter-sound correspondences, syllabication patterns, and morphology (e.g., roots and affixes) to read accurately unfamiliar multisyllabic words in context and out of context.* Ask students to list several syllabication patterns. Then generate numerical patterns that correspond to these same patterns. Use graphs or other mathematical models to analyze the patterns.

- *Mathematics Standard K.G.5. Model shapes in the world by building shapes from components (e.g., sticks and clay balls) and drawing shapes; and English Language Arts Standard SL.K.5. Add drawings or other visual displays to descriptions as desired to provide additional detail.* Have students create a model of a city by using various three-dimensional shapes to represent different objects. They should include an orthogonal drawing of the model showing the front, right side, and top views. Have them create a legend to demonstrate their use of shapes in the model. Finally, have them create a story about the city and illustrate it through photos, hand illustrations, or other visual displays.

Cross-disciplinary and integrated approaches are inherent in many research projects that students undertake. The writing demonstrates the capacity to build an argument, and the construction of mathematical models and analysis of data illustrate the capacity to interpret and transform ideas from graphic representations to verbal ones. By so doing, both English language arts and mathematics standards are addressed.

Differentiating Assessments to Encourage Higher Level Reasoning and Creativity

Although end-of-grade performance expectations are identified in the Common Core State Standards, teachers must also consider how differentiation of classroom assessments can be tailored to support the ongoing development of each student's mathematics abilities in order to meet gifted students' unique academic and social-emotional needs.

In mathematics, curriculum may be modified with more advanced, above-grade-level content (more difficult material, greater depth of exploration) and more challenging problems and projects that encourage students to stretch beyond their current level of performance through assessments that appropriately gauge the growth of advanced learners. Thus, product-based assessment is a crucial approach in this process. This should include authentic, unfamiliar problem solving and problem posing where students keep portfolios of exemplary work and research projects. Student interests should be taken into consideration for at least some of these problems and projects. Rubrics such as the one featured in Figure 3 might be used to encourage creativity as well as depth of understanding in problems and projects that are included in portfolios.

Assessment Criteria	1 Novice	2 Apprentice	3 Proficient	4 Distinguished
Depth of Understanding	Little or no understanding	Partial understanding; minor mathematical errors	Good understanding; mathematically correct	In-depth understanding; well-developed ideas
Fluency	One incomplete or unworkable strategy or technique	At least one appropriate solution with strategy or technique shown	At least two appropriate solutions; may use the same strategy or technique	Several appropriate solutions; may use the same strategy or technique
Flexibility	No method apparent	At least one method of solution (e.g., all graphs, all algebraic equations, and so on)	At least two methods of solution (e.g., geometric, graphical, algebraic, physical modeling)	Three or more methods of solution (e.g., geometric, graphical, algebraic, physical modeling)
Originality	Method may be different but does not lead to a solution	Method will lead to a solution but is fairly common	Unusual, workable method used by only a few students, or uncommon solution	Unique, insightful method or solution used only by one or two students
Elaboration or Elegance	Little or no appropriate explanation given	Explanation is understandable, but is unclear in some places	Clear explanation using correct mathematical terms	Clear, concise, precise explanations making good use of graphs, charts, models, or equations
Generalizations and Reasoning	No generalizations made, or they are incorrect and reasoning is unclear	At least one correct generalization made but not well-supported with clear reasoning	At least one well-made, supported generalization, or more than one correct but unsupported generalization	Several well-supported generalizations; clear reasoning
Extensions	No related mathematical question explored	At least one related mathematical question appropriately explored	One related question explored in-depth, or more than one question appropriately explored	More than one related question explored in-depth

Figure 3. Scoring rubric to encourage mathematical creativity. From "Creating and Developing Promising Young Mathematicians," by L. J. Sheffield, 2000, *Teaching Children Mathematics, 6,* p. 419. Copyright 2000 by the National Council of Teachers of Mathematics. Reprinted with permission from the National Council of Teachers of Mathematics. All rights reserved.

Ongoing formative and summative assessment should include embedded classroom assessments such as entry and exit slips and evaluation of student work during class. It is important to include challenging problems that can be solved on a variety of levels in different ways and that encourage extensions, creativity, and higher level reasoning to allow students to display and develop their mathematical talents. If standardized tests are used, they must have a high enough ceiling (e.g., problems above grade level) that they provide students the opportunity to exhibit mathematical expertise that goes beyond proficiency. Computer-assisted assessment that automatically adjusts the level of questions based on student responses might be used to identify growth and monitor continuous progress. Assessment of spatial abilities such as the ability to manipulate three-dimensional objects and mathematical creativity are also important for the development of STEM innovators. Fields such as engineering, surgery, and architecture, among others, require that students have highly developed spatial reasoning abilities, which are often overlooked in programs for the development of mathematical gifts and talents.

The purpose of assessment must also be considered. If it is used to determine participants in higher level opportunities, care must be taken to be as inclusive as possible and not to use the testing as a gatekeeper. In many instances, self-selection for advanced programs can be used quite successfully, assuming that courses and programs are not watered down for unprepared students.

Example assessments may be retrieved from the NCSM website (http://www.mathedleadership.org/ccss/itp/problem.html) and the Mathematics Assessment Project website (http://map.mathshell.org.uk/materials/index.php).

Talent Trajectory: Creating Pathways to Excellence in Mathematics

As noted in *Preparing the Next Generation of STEM Innovators*, "The long-term prosperity of our Nation will increasingly rely on talented and motivated individuals who will comprise the vanguard of scientific and technological innovations; every student in America deserves the opportunity to achieve his or her full potential" (National Science Board, 2010, p. v). Educators need to increase the levels of these promising mathematics students and not limit the numbers of students in advanced mathematics and specialized STEM programs. As noted previously, the NCTM Task Force on Mathematically Promising Students defined mathematical promise as a function of ability, motivation, belief, and experience or opportunity (Sheffield et al., 1999). This definition used the words "mathematical promise" deliberately in order to include students who traditionally had been identified as gifted and also to add students who traditionally had been excluded from rich mathematical opportunities that would allow for talent identification and development (Sheffield et al., 1999).

Whether students plan to enter a STEM field in a career ranging from astronaut to zoologist or simply to become well-informed citizens who can make sense of the world, recognize patterns, make generalizations and test conjectures, make and defend logical decisions, and critique the reasoning of others, mathematics is critical to their development. Some of the characteristics of thinking like a mathematician that teachers should encourage and develop in themselves and their students are:

- mathematical curiosity,
- creativity and innovation,
- enjoyment of patterns and puzzles,
- a growth mindset with confidence in their abilities to learn mathematics on a deeper level,
- willingness to take risks and increasingly difficult challenges, and
- perseverance in the face of failure.

Preparation of high-level STEM students should not be rushed. Appropriate pacing for our top students should include not only acceleration, but also time for students to experience the joy of investigating rich concepts in depth and applying innovative mathematical reasoning and justification to a variety of scientific, engineering, and other problems. They should have engaging, problem-based learning that allows students to grapple with mathematical challenges to deepen their understanding of complex concepts (Teague et al., 2011). There should be a seamless articulation from elementary to middle to high school, where courses are carefully planned and there is no repetition of courses or content within the courses, especially as students move from elementary to middle school or from middle school to high school. This should include flexibility in scheduling, location, seat time, and other potential impediments to ensure that students make continuous progress throughout the K–12 programs in those areas that hold great interest and appeal. For example, students who are interested in mathematics and preparing for STEM careers should have opportunities to take math every year of high school from highly motivated math teachers. There should be widespread availability of specialized STEM schools, programs, or classes for students from elementary through high school to fuel their passions and give them the preparation necessary to move ahead.

Before students take high school mathematics courses such as algebra, geometry, or integrated courses, they should master all of the critical areas of the sixth-, seventh-, and eighth-grade Common Core State Standards in a manner consistent with the Standards for Mathematical Practice, including the addition of a ninth standard focusing on innovation and creativity. However, many gifted students in mathematics should be prepared for rigorous high school courses by eighth grade or earlier, perhaps through a carefully constructed compacted or telescoped curriculum, and should be encouraged and have the opportunity to do so. A menu of options should be available for students following the first 3 years of high school mathematics. These options for advanced courses might include statistics, mathematical decision making, discrete mathematics, and calculus, and following the Standards for Mathematical Practice, courses should be designed to be challenging, engaging, and relevant, preparing students for and exciting them about their futures in college and careers. These courses may be provided at the high school, online, or through dual enrollment at a nearby college or university.

At the high school level, Appendix A of the Common Core State Standards for Mathematics (NGA & CCSSO, 2010b, p. 4) suggests either an integrated or a traditional pathway of courses for all students that may look like Figure 4.

Appendix A of the Common Core State Standards for Mathematics (NGA & CCSSO, 2010b) also includes sections on High School Mathematics in Middle School (p. 80), Middle School Acceleration (pp. 80–81), and Other Ways to Accelerate Students (p. 81). It then provides suggested outlines for a sequence of accelerated courses in either a traditional or an integrated pathway, beginning with accelerated seventh- and eighth-grade mathematics (pp. 82–146) and followed by suggestions for additional high school mathematics courses for advanced students (p. 147). The appendix writers acknowledged that students who take advanced courses in high school such as precalculus and calculus do better in college than students who do not, but warned against accelerating students into a watered-down algebra course in middle school and emphasized

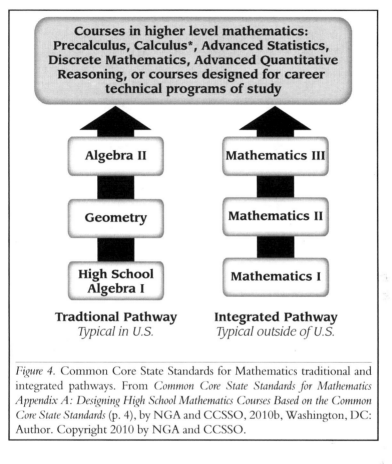

Courses in higher level mathematics: Precalculus, Calculus*, Advanced Statistics, Discrete Mathematics, Advanced Quantitative Reasoning, or courses designed for career technical programs of study

| Algebra II | Mathematics III |

| Geometry | Mathematics II |

| High School Algebra I | Mathematics I |

Tradtional Pathway
Typical in U.S.

Integrated Pathway
Typical outside of U.S.

Figure 4. Common Core State Standards for Mathematics traditional and integrated pathways. From *Common Core State Standards for Mathematics Appendix A: Designing High School Mathematics Courses Based on the Common Core State Standards* (p. 4), by NGA and CCSSO, 2010b, Washington, DC: Author. Copyright 2010 by NGA and CCSSO.

the importance of not skipping or rushing through critical foundational middle-grades content that increases the likelihood of success in later mathematics courses. They recommended a well-crafted sequence of compacted courses that use the Standards for Mathematical Practice. They also noted:

A menu of challenging options should be available for students after their third year of mathematics—and all students should be strongly encouraged to take mathematics in all years of high school. Traditionally, students taking high school mathematics in the eighth grade are expected to take Precalculus in their junior year and then

Calculus in their senior year. These recommendations allow for acceleration, but some students who are gifted and advanced in mathematics need more options at the middle and high school levels. Advanced courses might include Statistics, Discrete Mathematics, Mathematical Decision Making, or Mathematical Modeling. An array of challenging options will keep mathematics relevant for students, and give them a new set of tools for their futures in college and careers. (NGA & CCSSO, 2010b, p. 81)

Schools that may not have access to such an array of courses may want to consider connecting with mentors in the community or providing distance learning and online courses such as those offered by the Education Program for Gifted Youth (Stanford University), the Center for Talented Youth (Johns Hopkins University), TIP (Duke University), the Center for Talent Development (Northwestern University), and C-MITES (Carnegie-Mellon), among others.

It is also noted in Appendix A (NGA & CCSSO, 2010b) that care should be taken to provide opportunities for students who decide after middle school that they are interested in taking advanced mathematics such as AP Calculus and AP Statistics before leaving high school. NGA and CCSSO (2010b) noted that:

Additional opportunities for acceleration may include:
- Allowing students to take two mathematics courses simultaneously (such as Geometry and Algebra II, or Precalculus and Statistics).
- Allowing students in schools with block scheduling to take a mathematics course in both semesters of the same academic year.
- Offering summer courses that are designed to provide the equivalent experience of a full course in all regards, including attention to the Mathematical Practices.

- Creating different compaction ratios, including four years of high school content into three years beginning in 9th grade.
- Creating a hybrid Algebra II–Precalculus course that allows students to go straight to Calculus. (p. 81)

These recommendations are more in line with the acceleration research literature and position statements in gifted education that suggest intellectually talented youth achieve at an impressively high level if they receive an appropriately challenging education (Benbow & Stanley, 1996; Swiatek & Benbow, 1991, 1992). Moreover, accelerated students clearly excel in subsequent math courses and perform better than their equally able nonaccelerated peers (Brody & Benbow, 1987; Brody & Mills, 2005; Mills, Ablard, & Lynch, 1992). The National Association for Gifted Children's (2004) position statement on acceleration described research-based options such as "grade skipping, telescoping, early entrance into kindergarten or college, credit by examination, and acceleration in content areas" (para. 2) and concluded by stating, "highly able students with capability and motivation to succeed in placements beyond traditional age/ grade parameters should be provided the opportunity to enroll in appropriate classes and educational settings" (para. 7).

It is vital that educators develop the passion, expertise, motivation, and creativity of their most promising mathematics students. There are a number of extracurricular opportunities that can enhance this development. These opportunities should be in addition to—not in place of—engaging, challenging K–12 curricular mathematics programs. These extracurricular opportunities might include:

- participating in mathematical clubs and circles;
- obtaining mentorships and apprenticeships;
- entering math, science, and STEM competitions;
- conducting authentic scientific research;
- undertaking engineering design challenges; and
- engaging in online or other electronic experiences.

Implementing the Common Core State Standards With Various Program Models in Gifted Education

The models of delivery for advanced learners (or for any learner) are largely not addressed in the Common Core State Standards, allowing teachers and schools to implement services based on the needs of gifted students with the CCSS as a basis. Although gifted program design and delivery will be informed by these standards, programs and services for the gifted should be guided largely by assessment data about the abilities of students as well as best practices for serving them in each of the core subject areas.

As gifted program service models vary, so do the implementation implications for the CCSS. Gifted students receive services within heterogeneous settings, cluster-grouped classrooms, pull-out models, self-contained classrooms, and special schools.

Flexible Grouping in the Regular Classroom

For teachers of gifted and high-potential learners served in the heterogeneous, general education classroom with flexible grouping, the CCSS can serve as benchmarks for what all students should know, although educators should be careful not to limit curriculum for high-ability students based on the foundational expectations that would be provided to general education learners. In fact, those who are advanced may show mastery of content standards much sooner than other learners (NGA & CCSSO, 2010a). As the CCSS authors acknowledge the limited nature of the standards in addressing the needs of the gifted, teachers must then modify learning experiences for these students.

To address the curricular needs of gifted and high-potential students, teachers can differentiate curriculum through using pre- and formative assessments and compacting or accelerating the curriculum, posing progressively more complex issues, adjusting or replacing texts according to each student's reading level and interest, modifying mathematical processes according to those previously mastered, and pacing instruction according to individual rates of learning. Although the CCSS provide indicators of general levels of performance for all students, teachers will need to modify learning so that gifted learners are provided appropriately challenging, stimulating experiences throughout the instructional day for continued progress. The need for authentically challenging activities for advanced students in mathematics is not to be underestimated, as it links closely with student interest, which ultimately translates to lifelong pursuits in mathematics.

Cluster Grouping

In cluster-grouped classrooms, teachers can use the CCSS as a basis for preassessment to determine where students are performing and adjust grouping according to students' abilities, interests, and strengths with respect to mathematics. Teachers can group high-ability students flexibly throughout the school day to allow students the opportunity to regularly engage with peers of similar abilities and interests according to individual mathematical skills addressed in the CCSS or by a combination of skills.

Pull-Out Models

Teachers who serve gifted students in pull-out models, where gifted students spend a portion of their school day (or week) in a setting other than their general education classroom, are encouraged to consider how the activities in the pull-out setting offer advanced learning experiences in mathematics that are beyond those that would be provided in the general education classroom. Along with other methods of differentiation, such as providing for greater depth, complexity, and critical thinking opportunities, teachers are encouraged to use ongoing assessment information, including preassessments, to accommodate for the differences in mathematical ability between and among the students in the pull-out program.

Self-Contained

Gifted students who are served throughout the school day with gifted peers in self-contained classrooms engage in a range of mathematical experiences as different content areas are addressed. Although teachers of the gifted in these classrooms use the CCSS as a foundation for setting grade-level expectations, they also consider gifted learners with advanced skills in mathematics who often evidence proficiency in foundational skills early in the school year or at a pace that is faster than general education peers or even their gifted education peers. Thus, appropriate grouping within the self-contained classroom is recommended according to literacy and mathematical abilities. The curriculum should be qualitatively different from the curriculum offered to general education students according to the needs of individual students in terms of rate of learning, depth of content, difficulty of products, and complexity of thinking processes.

Special Schools

Special schools for gifted students are available for both elementary and secondary students. In general, the curriculum offered is both accelerated and enriched to provide accommodations for students who can handle work that is significantly more advanced than what is typical for their age-mates. Although these schools serve only students with gifts and talents and the curriculum offerings tend to be advanced, it is still vital that school personnel go beyond simply using the CCSS for a higher grade level when creating or aligning curriculum. Keeping in mind the natural progression of knowledge and skills, specialized schools must be certain that addressing any gaps in knowledge resulting from radical acceleration is a priority, particularly when students are pulled to the specialized school from many different educational settings. Despite the fact that the entire school is focused on students who spend their school day interacting with their intellectual peers, all of the gifted students in any particular class are not alike in their need for a different pace and differentiation in the complexity of the material being taught. For example, mathematically advanced students may vary in their mathematical abilities; they also may not be advanced in other content areas. The Common Core State Standards are an important tool to use in determining how to accommodate individual needs within a class, not only in mathematics but also in English language arts.

Other than specialized schools, most of the programming options discussed above are used primarily at the elementary and middle school levels, but there is no reason that these cannot be used at the secondary level, too. Because upper level coursework is highly specialized, educators may believe that those who take such courses are advanced to the same degree. Simply because students are studying differential equations at the 10th-grade level does not mean that all students in the class are able to handle the same level of abstraction or can keep up with a fast pace. The CCSS can be used as a guideline to spur the necessary accommodations by looking across the standards for material to advance to the next level of learning.

Alignment of the Common Core State Standards With the Gifted Education Programming Standards

This booklet, designed around the Common Core State Standards for Mathematics for use by teachers with gifted learners, was developed in alignment with both 21st century skills (Partnership for 21st Century Skills, n.d.) and the 2010 NAGC Pre-K–Grade 12 Gifted Programming Standards in key areas and is connected and integrated in important ways to multiple professional communities within gifted education and also across general education.

The NAGC Pre-K–Grade 12 Gifted Programming Standards represent the professional standards for programs in gifted education across P–12 levels. Within these standards, the curriculum and assessment standards were used to design the mathematics booklet in the following ways:

- *Development of scope and sequence*: This booklet has demonstrated a set of interrelated emphases/activities for use across K–12, with a common format and within key content domains.
- *Use of differentiation strategies*: The booklet developers used the central differentiation strategies emphasized in the

standards, including critical and creative thinking, problem solving, inquiry, research, and concept development.

- *Use of appropriate pacing/acceleration techniques, including pre-assessment, formative assessment, and pacing*: The booklet developers used all of these strategies as well as more advanced, innovative, and complex mathematics to ensure the challenge level for gifted learners.

- *Adaptation or replacement of the core curriculum*: The project extends the Common Core State Standards by ensuring that gifted learners master them and then go beyond them in key ways. Some standards are mastered earlier (e.g., basic computation skills and algorithms), and others are practiced consistently throughout the curriculum such as problem solving, problem posing, and skill and concept development.

- *Use of culturally sensitive curriculum approaches leading to cultural competency*: The booklet developers have employed mathematics problems and research on learning mathematics from around the world to ensure that students have an appreciation for the contributions of different cultures to mathematics.

- *Use of research-based materials*: The booklet developers have included models and techniques found to be highly effective with gifted learners in enhancing critical thinking, mathematical reasoning and sense-making, problem solving, and innovation. They have also used the discourse and questioning techniques found in *Project M²: Mentoring Young Mathematicians* (Gavin, Casa, Chapin, & Sheffield, 2010) and *Project M³: Mentoring Mathematical Minds* (Gavin et al., 2008), both research-based mathematics programs that are used nationally for gifted and advanced learners.

- *Use of metacognitive strategies*: The booklet developers included activities where students use reflection, planning, monitoring, and assessing skills.

- *Talent development in areas of aptitude and interest in various domains (cognitive, affective, aesthetic)*: The booklet presents examples that provide multiple opportunities for students to explore domain-specific interests such as conducting research, investigating problems, creating models, and participating in competitions, thereby exercising multiple levels of skills in cognitive, affective, and aesthetic areas.

Implications for Professional Learning When Implementing the Common Core State Standards

Professional learning is essential for all educators to increase effectiveness and results for students (Learning Forward, 2011). Teachers and content specialists should collaborate in learning communities to identify specific knowledge and skills needed to serve different groups of learners. As schools and school districts adopt and begin using the Common Core State Standards, all educators should be involved in a variety of ongoing learning options, including job-embedded professional development to address the needs of gifted and high-potential students. All educators need a repertoire of research-supported strategies to deliberately adapt and modify curriculum, instruction, and assessment within the framework of the CCSS, based on the needs of gifted students as well as those with high potential.

Although the CCSS provide the framework for the learning experiences for all students, gifted educators need focused training that is content-specific for differentiating the standards (VanTassel-Baska et al., 2008). Systematic professional learning will support all educators to adapt or modify the CCSS based on the needs of the learner. To differentiate effectively for gifted and high-potential learners, all educators need to develop expertise at designing learning experiences and assessments that are conceptually advanced, challenging, and complex.

Professional learning for implementing the CCSS for gifted and high-potential learners should focus on evidence-based differentiation and instructional practices as they relate to specific core content. The training should demonstrate how and when to apply acceleration strategies; how to add depth and complexity elements such as critical thinking, creative thinking, problem solving, and inquiry; and how to develop and encourage innovation, all within the CCSS. In addition to the curriculum adaptation and modification, the professional learning experiences should also demonstrate content-specific ways to design and implement differentiated product-based assessments as well as pre- and postassessments appropriate for advanced students. However, gifted educators are in no way expected to be experts in all content areas; therefore, it is imperative to develop collaborative relations with skilled content specialists to provide knowledgeable advice, content-specific peer coaching services, and pedagogical knowledge while implementing the CCSS.

Examples of Professional Learning Models for Implementing the CCSS

Educators should take an active role in designing options to facilitate their learning and improvement of student results (Learning Forward, 2011). Active learning may include any of the following elements:

- discussion and dialogue,
- coaching and modeling,
- demonstration and reflection,
- inquiry and problem solving, and
- a tiered model of professional learning experiences (Learning Forward, 2011).

Discussion and dialogue. A professional learning community (PLC) of 3–6 teachers may agree to work together to improve their practice and student results (Lieberman & Miller, 2008). The PLC would identify specific learning standards for its grade and subject within the CCSS. Through regularly scheduled meetings, the group of teachers would share ideas on ways to teach the standard, including ideas for differentiating learning experiences for advanced learners. The teachers of the PLC would identify strategies from the discussions, implement them in their classrooms, and then share their experiences when the group meets again. Ideally, the PLC would have collaboration and support from a gifted education specialist to provide ideas and resources for studying and practicing effective differentiation for gifted students.

Coaching and modeling. Learning options can include collaborative relationships such as mentoring or coaching. Specifically, peer coaching as a form of job-embedded professional development provides teachers a natural support system that can enhance teacher performance by the privileged sharing of knowledge and expertise through collaboration (Little & Ayers, 2011). Whether it is the gifted educator serving as a peer coach or the one being coached, the coach may assume various roles, including content expert, classroom helper, teacher observer, and instructional facilitator (Cotabish & Robinson, 2012; Dailey, Cotabish, & Robinson, in press).

Demonstration and reflection. Demonstrations are a great way for teachers to learn new practices within authentic contexts. Professional learning leaders (Learning Forward, 2011) can work with teachers to demonstrate differentiation strategies within the CCSS. Examples of this model may include a teacher who is skillfully using preassessment to diagnose learner readiness and providing differentiated tasks based on the results. The organizer of the professional learning would arrange for teacher learners to observe the demonstration one or more times and then practice the strategy in their classrooms. Ultimately the active demonstration strategy is enhanced by reflection on what was learned and how the implementation improved student engagement and performance.

Inquiry and problem solving. Inquiry and problem solving are techniques involving action research by a teacher or team of teachers. In the action research process, teachers examine their own educational practice systematically and carefully using techniques of research. The inquiry conducted by the teacher or team will generate data to inform or change teaching practices. One of the primary benefits of an action research approach to professional learning is the immediacy and proximity of the inquiry within the expected content of the curriculum. For instance, a teacher or a group of teachers may decide to study the effects of providing differentiated mathematics problems, projects, and instruction to advanced learners. Research techniques of measurement and consistent implementation would guide the inquiry with baseline assessment data for all students in the intervention as well as a control group if one is available. The teacher would implement the intervention, differentiated mathematics instruction, over a determined period of time and follow it with posttesting to look for changes in student achievement (within-subjects) or differences compared to the group without the intervention (between-subjects). Frequently, professional learning specialists help teachers develop ideas and data collection techniques for inquiry and problem solving.

A tiered model of professional learning experiences. In a tiered model of professional learning, the school or school district establishes clear expectations for developing expertise in gifted education and differentiated instruction (Johnsen, Kettler, & Lord, 2011). For gifted education professionals, the model would be built around the NAGC-CEC National Standards for Gifted Education Professional Development (Kitano, Montgomery, VanTassel-Baska, & Johnsen, 2008). Leaders within the school or school district would develop seminar learning experiences in which teachers would come together to learn differentiation strategies according to these tiered expectations (e.g., novice, intermediate, advanced). Experts in subject-specific differentiation would discuss and demonstrate specific ways to differentiate the CCSS across grade levels. These seminars would prepare teachers in specific content domains (e.g., mathematics) to practice evidence-based strategies for differentiating the CCSS for advanced learners. As teachers acquire expertise, they gradually move up the tiers from novice to intermediate to expert. As they reach expert levels, they begin to model the expertise and lead seminars with other teachers in their content area. The key ingredient is to provide clear guidelines of the skills expected to develop expertise in differentiating with the CCSS.

Collaboration With General and Special Education

It cannot be emphasized enough that gifted education professionals must collaborate with other educational partners and not "go it alone" in the process of implementing the Common Core State Standards on behalf of advanced learners and their talent development process. Gifted educators' roles include direct service and advocacy for the gifted child, including academic, social, and emotional development. It is important to recognize that giftedness impacts the development of the whole child, which involves both external and internal factors. Numerous partners need to be involved in the collaboration process, depending on the specific needs and abilities of the child.

First, content experts must be included in any discussion. When examining trajectories in mathematics, it is critical that experts in these subject areas be involved in the process. Although gifted education specialists have significant training and expertise in strategy instruction, they must link to those people who have passion and expertise in the content areas so that students with promise and talent receive appropriate levels of instruction that are not tied to age or grade considerations.

Second, parents and families must be included in the collaboration process. Although schools and educators play a critical role in the process of talent development, there is an equally important role of outside clubs, competitions, and community opportunities. Parents clearly play a role in mediating the selection and promotion of skills and activities in which students can engage. Parents must be perceived as both a source and a recipient of pertinent information, as well as partners in the educational process.

Third, people from outside entities that promote specific content emphases must be approached as partners in the educational process. These entities can include online communities, colleges and universities, and different competition and contest organizations. Individuals affiliated with professional organizations might also provide connections to students and are valuable collaborators to facilitate talent development in a specific career pathway.

Fourth, when working with gifted students from diverse and special populations, gifted educators must collaborate with professionals who advocate and provide services for other special groups of students. Educators from special education (including ELL programs) and poverty-related programs play key roles in the development of talent in gifted children who are impacted by other factors within their lives.

Last—and this is very critical—within their roles as gatekeepers and managers of the entire educational process, administrators must be included in discussions of systemic talent development. Rather than making talent development a highly individualistic, ad-hoc process, administrators play a key role in systematizing an educational program that can provide progression within the disciplines for talented students.

A Possible Timeline for Implementing the Common Core State Standards Locally

Implementation of the Common Core State Standards at the K–12 level encompasses several varied but necessary tasks (see Table 1). For example, in mathematics, both the Standards for Mathematical Practice addressing process and proficiencies and the Standards for Mathematical Content must be taken together as a way in which educators can develop mathematical practitioners and mathematical experts, not just proficient math students. A first step toward implementation is to become familiar with both sets of standards. Second, look at current practices, analyzing them to determine if there are gaps between current practices and practices that would reflect the CCSS. Next, provide all teachers with professional development that is targeted on best practices in math and with gifted students. Where gaps have been identified, teachers then adjust content, process, products, and assessments to reflect the new mathematics standards, bearing in mind that student outcomes should be aimed at developing expertise. Gather resources and consult with content specialists and gifted education specialists to assist with realignment. Consider the 2010 NAGC Pre-K–Grade 12 Gifted Programming Standards in the realignment process. Make sure

Table 1
A Sample Timeline for Implementation of the CCSS

Task	Person(s) Responsible	When
Know and understand the CCSS for Mathematics.	All school personnel	August–September
Gather evidence to determine the extent to which current practices reflect the practice standards; identify gaps in practice and/or content.	Teacher representatives at each grade level, building-level administrators, gifted specialist	October–December
Gather evidence to determine the extent to which current content reflects the content standards; identify gaps in practice and/or content.	Teacher representatives at each grade level, building-level administrators, gifted specialist, math specialist	October–December
Provide professional development to identify best practices in teaching math and adapting the CCSS for students with gifts and talents.	All teachers	January–March
Make adjustments to practices and content to reflect gaps that were identified, deleting curriculum that is not rigorous and does not meet the standards.	All teachers	January–March
Gather resources and assist with realignment to CCSS and to gifted education programming standards.	Gifted specialist, building-level administrator, math specialist, other necessary personnel	January–March
Provide professional development to prepare all teachers for full implementation of the CCSS for gifted and high-potential students.	Gifted specialist, building-level administrator, math specialist, other necessary personnel	April–July
Provide ongoing support for full implementation.	Gifted specialist, building-level administrator, math specialist, other necessary personnel	August–July

the curriculum that is developed is coherent and is focused on the development of concepts, not add-on activities. Provide professional development to ensure that school personnel understand the new standards and the changes needed to implement them for gifted and high-potential students.

Resources to Assist With the Implementation Process

There are a variety of resources that can assist university personnel, administrators, and coordinators of gifted programs at state and local levels in implementing the new CCSS for gifted learners, including assessments that measure the depth and breadth of a student's knowledge within a domain of talent development; curriculum units of study that are already differentiated and research-based; instructional strategies that employ the use of higher order thinking skills; and programming options that include appropriate pacing, rigor, innovation, and extended learning beyond the classroom.

The 2010 NAGC Pre-K–Grade 12 Gifted Programming Standards should be used as a tool to understand the elements that a differentiated curriculum for the gifted learner would include. For university personnel, it would be helpful to review the Teacher Preparation Standards in Gifted Education (NAGC & CEC, 2006) to see the extent to which there is alignment to the new CCSS.

What follows is a sampling of resources that might be considered in implementing the CCSS with gifted students.

Assessment

Johnsen, S. K. (Ed.). (2012). *NAGC Pre-K–Grade 12 Gifted Education Programming Standards: A guide to planning and implementing high-quality services.* Waco, TX: Prufrock Press.

Sulak, T. N., & Johnsen, S. K. (2012). Assessments for measuring student outcomes. In S. K. Johnsen (Ed.), *NAGC Pre-K–Grade 12 Gifted Education Programming Standards: A guide to planning and implementing high-quality services* (pp. 283–306). Waco, TX: Prufrock Press.

Assessments for measuring the progress of gifted and talented students may be found in the *NAGC Pre-K–Grade 12 Gifted Education Programming Standards: A Guide to Planning and Implementing High-Quality Services* (Johnsen, 2012). Sulak and Johnsen (2012) described informal assessments that can be used informally in assessing student outcomes in creativity, critical thinking, curriculum, interests, learning and motivation, and social-emotional areas. They have also identified specific product and performance assessments and other assessments that might be useful in program planning and evaluation. Although many of the assessments do not have technical information, 23 do provide either reliability or validity information.

Partnership for Assessment of Readiness for College and Careers
   The Partnership for Assessment of Readiness for College and Careers (PARCC) is a 24-state consortium that has been formed to develop a common assessment system to measure the CCSS. To learn more about its work and the progress of its assessment development, visit http://www.parcconline.org/about-parcc.

Robins, J. H., & Jolly, J. L. (2011). Technical information regarding assessment. In S. K. Johnsen (Ed.), *Identifying gifted students: A practical guide* (2nd ed., pp. 75–188). Waco, TX: Prufrock Press.

Information regarding standardized achievement tests may be found in *Identifying Gifted Students: A Practical Guide* (Robins

& Jolly, 2011). In their chapter, Robins and Jolly provided a list of 28 instruments that are frequently used in the identification of gifted students and their technical qualities. Because many of these assessments are also used to identify students who are above grade level in specific academic areas, they would be appropriate for measuring a gifted student's academic progress.

Smarter Balanced Assessment Consortium

Smarter Balanced Assessment Consortium is a state-led consortium working to develop assessments that are aligned to the CCSS. The web-based resources include the alignment of the CCSS to International Baccalaureate, the Texas College Career Readiness Standards, depth of knowledge, and breadth of coverage within a domain. To learn more about the consortium, alignments with other standards, and the consortium's progress on developing assessments for the standards, visit http://educationnorthwest.org/resource/1331 and http://www.smarterbalanced.org/resources-events/publications-resources. Note that it offers sample assessment items for seventh- and eighth-grade mathematics standards, and these might be useful to determine whether all students have mastered the CCSS for middle school before proceeding on to high school mathematics courses.

Curriculum and Instructional Strategies

Carnegie Mellon Institute for Talented Elementary and Secondary Students

The Carnegie Mellon Institute for Talented Elementary and Secondary Students (C-MITES) offers resources and links to curriculum in mathematics, science, technology, engineering, language arts, and social studies. For more information, visit http://www.cmu.edu/cmites.

Center for Gifted Education at The College of William and Mary

The Center for Gifted Education at The College of William and Mary has designed curricular units in the areas of mathematics, language arts, science, and social studies that are based on the three dimensions of the Integrated Curriculum Model: advanced content, higher level processes and products, and interdisciplinary concepts, issues, and themes. The materials emphasize a sophistication of ideas, opportunities for extensions, the use of higher order thinking skills, and opportunities for student exploration based on interest. Specific teaching strategies are also described on the website, including literature webs, the Hamburger Model for Persuasive Writing, a vocabulary web, the use of Paul's Elements of Reasoning, analyzing primary sources, and a research model for students. For more information about the units, visit the Center for Gifted Education at http://education.wm.edu/centers/cfge/curriculum/index.php.

Davidson Institute for Talent Development

The Davidson Institute for Talent Development offers links to resources in mathematics, language arts, science, social studies, arts and culture, and related domains. It also provides links to information about educational options such as ability grouping, acceleration, enrichment programs, competitions, and other services. To explore these resources, visit http://www.davidson-gifted.org/db/browse_by_topic_resources.aspx.

Kendall Hunt's *Math Innovations*

Math Innovations: Moving Math Forward Through Critical Thinking and Exploration provides a complete middle-grades math curricula for all students and a compacted, 2-year sequence for advanced students that addresses the CCSS and prepares students to take high school mathematics courses while in middle school without skipping any of the critical middle school mathematics standards. For more information, visit http://www.kendallhunt.com/mathinnovations.

National Council of Supervisors of Mathematics and National Council of Teachers of Mathematics

The National Council of Supervisors of Mathematics (http://www.mathedleadership.org/ccss/index.html) and the National Council of Teachers of Mathematics (http://www.nctm.org) both have curricula, assessment, and instructional resources for implementing the CCSS for all students, along with recommendations for a research agenda related to the standards.

Neag Center for Gifted Education and Talent Development

The Neag Center for Gifted Education and Talent Development offers online resources that describe research studies and defensible practices in the field of gifted and talented education. Some of the studies address curriculum at the high school level, the explicit teaching of thinking skills, cluster grouping, algebraic understanding, reading with young children, differentiated performance assessments, and content-based curriculum. To access the studies, visit http://www.gifted.uconn.edu/nrcgt/nrconlin.html.

Project M^2: Mentoring Young Mathematicians

Project M^2: Mentoring Young Mathematicians provides differentiated units in mathematics for grades K–2 that focus on geometry and measurement at the primary level and engage students in critical and creative thinking and problem solving. For more information regarding the project, visit http://www.projectm2.org.

Project M^3: Mentoring Mathematical Minds

Project M^3: Mentoring Mathematical Minds provides differentiated units in mathematics for grades 2–6 that focus on algebraic reasoning, number and computation, probability and statistics, and geometry and measurement and engage students in critical and creative thinking and problem solving. For more information regarding the project, visit http://www.projectm3.org.

Tools for the Common Core State Standards

This blog from one of the authors of the Common Core State Standards provides news about tools that are being developed to support the standards' implementation. For more information, visit http://commoncoretools.me.

Gifted Education Programming

Colorado Department of Education

The Colorado Department of Education provides *Gifted Education Guidelines and Resources* in programming for gifted and talented students that describe differentiated instruction for gifted learners (e.g., acceleration, content extension, higher order thinking skills), content options to address identified areas of strength, advanced learning plans, and acceleration tables. To retrieve the resources, visit http://www.cde.state.co.us/gt/resources.htm.

Institute for Research and Policy on Acceleration

This website features *A Nation Deceived: How Schools Hold Back America's Brightest Students*, a two-part report that provides research-based information about acceleration and examines current practices. To download the entire report, visit http://www.accelerationinstitute.org/Nation_Deceived/Get_Report.aspx.

References

Barnett, L. B., & Durden, W. G. (1993). Education patterns of academically talented youth. *Gifted Child Quarterly, 37,* 161–168.

Benbow, C. P., & Stanley, J. C. (1996). Inequity in equity: How current educational equity policies place able students at risk. *Psychology, Public Policy, and Law, 2,* 249–293.

Bressoud, D. M. (2009). Is the sky still falling? *Notices of the AMS, 56,* 20–25.

Brody, L. (2004). *Grouping and acceleration practices in gifted education.* Thousand Oaks, CA: Corwin Press.

Brody, L. E., & Benbow, C. P. (1987). Accelerative strategies: How effective are they for the gifted? *Gifted Child Quarterly, 31,* 105–110.

Brody, L. E., & Mills, C. J. (2005). Talent search research: What have we learned? *High Ability Studies, 16,* 97–111.

Chapin, S. H., O'Connor, C., & Anderson, N. C. (2009). *Classroom discussions: Using math talk to help students learn.* Sausalito, CA: Math Solutions.

Colangelo, N., Assouline, S. G., & Gross, M. U. M. (2004). *A nation deceived: How schools hold back America's brightest students*

(Vol. 1). Iowa City: The University of Iowa, The Connie Belin & Jacqueline N. Blank International Center for Gifted Education and Talent Development. Retrieved from http://www.accelerationinstitute.org/nation_deceived

Cotabish, A., & Robinson, A. (2012). The effects of peer coaching on the evaluation knowledge, skills, and concerns of gifted program administrators. *Gifted Child Quarterly, 56,* 160–170. doi:10.1177/0016986212446861

Council of Chief State School Officers. (2011). *InTASC model core teaching standards: A resource for state dialogue.* Retrieved from http://www.ccsso.org/resources/programs/interstate_teacher_assessment_consortium_%28intasc%29.html

Dailey, D., Cotabish, A., & Robinson, A. (in press). Peer coaching in the elementary science classroom: A catalyst for success. *TEMPO.*

Gavin, M. K., Casa, T. M., Adelson, J. L., Carroll, S. R., & Sheffield, L. J (2009). The impact of advanced curriculum on the achievement of mathematically promising elementary students. *Gifted Child Quarterly, 53,* 188–202.

Gavin, M. K, Casa, T. M., Chapin, S. H., & Sheffield, L. J. (2010). *Project M²: Mentoring young mathematicians.* Dubuque, IA: Kendall Hunt.

Gavin, M. K, Chapin, S. H., Dailey, J., & Sheffield, L. J. (2008). *Project M³: Mentoring mathematical minds.* Dubuque, IA: Kendall Hunt.

Gavin, M. K., Dailey, J., Chapin, S. H., & Sheffield, L. J. (2008). *Getting into shapes.* Dubuque, IA: Kendall Hunt.

Gavin, M. K., & Sheffield, L. J. (2010). Using curriculum to develop mathematical promise in the middle grades. In M. Saul, S. Assouline, & L. J. Sheffield (Eds.), *The peak in the middle: Developing mathematically gifted students in the middle grades* (pp. 51–76). Reston, VA: National Council of Teachers of Mathematics.

Gavin, M. K., Sheffield, L. J., Dailey, J., & Chapin, S. H. (2008). *Treasures from the attic: Exploring fractions.* Dubuque, IA: Kendall Hunt.

Gross, M. U. M. (2006). Exceptionally gifted children: Long-term outcomes of academic acceleration and nonacceleration. *Journal for the Education of the Gifted, 29,* 404–429.

Heck, D. J., Weiss, I. R., & Pasley, J. D. (2011). *A priority research agenda for understanding the influence of the Common Core State Standards for Mathematics.* Retrieved from http://www.horizon-research.com/reports/2011/CCSSMresearchagenda/research_agenda.php

Johnsen, S. K., Kettler, T., & Lord, E. W. (2011, November). *Using the 2010 NAGC Pre-K–Grade 12 Gifted Programming Standards in professional development.* Paper presented at the annual meeting of the National Association for Gifted Children, New Orleans, LA.

Karp, A. (2010). Inspiring and developing student interest: Several examples from foreign schools. In M. Saul, S. Assouline, & L. J. Sheffield (Eds.), *The peak in the middle: Developing mathematically gifted students in the middle grades* (pp. 171–185). Reston, VA: National Council of Teachers of Mathematics.

Kilpatrick, J., Swafford, J., & Findell, B. (2001). *Adding it up: Helping children learn mathematics.* Washington, DC: National Academy Press.

Kitano, M., Montgomery, D., VanTassel-Baska, J., & Johnsen, S. K. (2008). *Using the national gifted education standards for preK–12 professional development.* Thousand Oaks, CA: Corwin Press.

Kolitch, E. R., & Brody, L. E. (1992). Mathematics acceleration of highly talented students: An evaluation. *Gifted Child Quarterly, 36,* 78–86.

Krutetskii, V. A. (1976). *The psychology of mathematical abilities in schoolchildren* (J. Teller, Trans.). Chicago, IL: University of Chicago Press. (Original work published in 1968)

Learning Forward. (2011). *Standards for Professional Learning: Learning communities.* Retrieved from http://www.learningforward.org/standards/learningcommunities/index.cfm

Lieberman, A., & Miller, L. (Eds.). (2008). *Teachers in professional communities.* New York, NY: Teachers College Press.

Little, C., & Ayers, C. (2011). Professional development to support successful curriculum implementation. In J. VanTassel-Baska & C. Little (Eds.), *Content-based curriculum for the gifted* (2nd ed., pp. 413–436). Waco, TX: Prufrock Press.

Mathematical Association of America, & National Council of Teachers of Mathematics. (2012). *MAA/NCTM position paper on calculus.* Retrieved from http://www.nctm.org/about/content.aspx?id=32351

Mills, C. J., Ablard, K. E., & Lynch, S. J. (1992). Academically talented students' preparation for advanced-level coursework after individually-paced precalculus class. *Journal for the Education of the Gifted, 16,* 3–17.

National Assessment of Educational Progress. (2011). *NAEP mathematics framework.* Retrieved from http://nces.ed.gov/nationsreportcard/mathematics/whatmeasure.asp

National Association for Gifted Children. (2004). *NAGC position paper on acceleration.* Retrieved from http://www.nagc.org/index.aspx?id=383

National Association for Gifted Children. (2006). *NAGC research base to support the NAGC-CEC teacher preparation standards in gifted education.* Retrieved from http://www.nagc.org/index.aspx?id=1880

National Association for Gifted Children. (2010). *NAGC Pre-K–Grade 12 Gifted Programming Standards.* Retrieved from http://www.nagc.org/ProgrammingStandards.aspx

National Association for Gifted Children, & Council for Exceptional Children. (2006). *NAGC-CEC Teacher Knowledge and Skill Standards for gifted and talented education.* Retrieved from http://www.nagc.org/NCATEStandards.aspx

National Center for Education Statistics. (2007). *Trends in International Mathematics and Science Study (TIMSS).* Retrieved from http://nces.ed.gov/timss

National Council of Supervisors of Mathematics. (2011). *Improving student achievement by expanding opportunities for our most promising students of mathematics.* Retrieved from http://www.mathedleadership.org/resources/position.html

National Council of Teachers of Mathematics. (1980). *An agenda for action: Recommendations for school mathematics*. Reston, VA: Author.

National Council of Teachers of Mathematics. (2000). *Principles and Standards for School Mathematics*. Retrieved from http://illuminations.nctm.org/Standards.aspx

National Council of Teachers of Mathematics, National Council of Supervisors of Mathematics, Association of State Supervisors of Mathematics, & Association of Mathematics Teacher Educators. (2010). *Mathematics education organizations unite to support implementation of Common Core State Standards*. Retrieved from http://www.nctm.org/uploadedFiles/Research_News_and_Advocacy/Common_Core_Standards/CCSS_JointStatement20100601.pdf

National Governors Association Center for Best Practices, & Council of Chief State School Officers. (2010a). *Common Core State Standards for Mathematics*. Retrieved from http://www.corestandards.org/the-standards

National Governors Association Center for Best Practices, & Council of Chief State School Officers. (2010b). *Common Core State Standards for Mathematics Appendix A: Designing high school mathematics courses based on the Common Core State Standards*. Retrieved from http://www.corestandards.org/assets/CCSSI_Mathematics_Appendix_A.pdf

National Science Board. (2010). *Preparing the next generation of STEM innovators: Identifying and developing our nation's human capital*. Retrieved from http://www.nsf.gov/nsb/publications/2010/nsb1033.pdf

Partnership for 21st Century Skills. (n.d.). *Framework for 21st century learning*. Retrieved from http://www.p21.org/overview

Rothery, T. G. (2008). High school mathematics: Why the rush? *Mathematics Teacher, 102,* 324–325.

Rusczyk. R. (2012). *The calculus trap*. Retrieved from http://www.artofproblemsolving.com/Resources/articles.php?page=calculustrap

Sheffield, L. J. (2000). Creating and developing promising young mathematicians. *Teaching Children Mathematics, 6,* 416–419, 426.

Sheffield, L. J. (2003). *Extending the challenge in mathematics: Developing mathematical promise in K–8 students.* Thousand Oaks, CA: Corwin Press.

Sheffield, L. J. (2006, March). Developing mathematical promise and creativity. *Journal of the Korea Society of Mathematical Education Series D: Research in Mathematical Education 10,* 1–11.

Sheffield, L. J., Bennett, J., Berriozabal, M., DeArmond, M., & Wertheimer, R. (1999). Report of the Task Force on the Mathematically Promising. In L. J. Sheffield (Ed.), *Developing mathematically promising students* (pp. 309–316). Reston, VA: National Council of Teachers of Mathematics.

Sheffield, L. J., Chapin, S. H., & Gavin, M. K. (2010a). *Notable numbers: Focusing on fractions, decimals and percents.* Dubuque, IA: Kendall Hunt.

Sheffield, L. J., Chapin, S. H., & Gavin, M. K. (2010b). *Sizing up shapes.* Dubuque, IA: Kendall Hunt.

Subotnik, R., Edmiston, A., & Rayhack, K. (2007). Developing national policies in STEM talent development: Obstacle and opportunities. In P. Csermely, K. Korlevic, & K. Sulyok (Eds.), *Science education: Models and networking of student research training under 21* (pp. 28–38). Amsterdam, the Netherlands: IOS Press.

Swiatek, M. A. (1993). A decade of longitudinal research on academic acceleration through the Study of Mathematically Precocious Youth. *Roeper Review, 15,* 120–123.

Swiatek, M. A., & Benbow, C. P. (1991). A ten-year longitudinal follow-up of ability matched accelerated and unaccelerated gifted students. *Journal of Educational Psychology, 83,* 528–538.

Swiatek, M. A., & Benbow, C. P. (1992). Nonacademic correlates of satisfaction with accelerative programs. *Journal of Youth and Adolescence, 21,* 699–723.

Teague, D., Avineri, T., Belledin, C., Graves, J., Noble, R., Hernandez, M., & Robinson, D. (2011). Issues of equity for advanced students. In M. Strutchens & J. R. Quander (Eds.), *Focus in high school mathematics: Fostering reasoning and sense making for all students* (pp. 65–84). Reston, VA: National Council of Teachers of Mathematics.

VanTassel-Baska, J., Feng, A., Brown, E., Bracken, B., Stambaugh, T., & French, H. (2008) A study of differentiated instructional change over three years. *Gifted Child Quarterly, 52*, 297–312.

Warshauer, M., McCabe, T., Sorto, M., Strickland, S., Warshauer, H., & White, A. (2010). Equity. In M. Saul, S. Assouline, & L. J. Sheffield (Eds.), *The peak in the middle: Developing mathematically gifted students in the middle grades* (pp. 155–170). Reston, VA: National Council of Teachers of Mathematics.

Appendix A
Definitions of Key Terms

Acceleration is a broad term used to describe ways in which gifted student learning may occur at a fast and appropriate rate throughout the years of schooling. It refers to content acceleration through preassessment, compacting, and reorganizing curriculum by unit or year; grade skipping; telescoping 2 years into one; dual enrollment in high school and college or university; and more personalized approaches such as tutorials, mentorships, and independent research that also would be sensitive to the advanced starting level of these learners for instruction. Both Advanced Placement (AP) and International Baccalaureate (IB) at the high school level represent programs of study already accelerated in content. AP courses also may be taken on a fast-track schedule earlier as appropriate.

Appropriate pacing refers to the rate at which material is taught to advanced learners. Because they are often capable of mastering new material more rapidly than typical learners, appropriate pacing would involve careful preassessment to determine readiness for more advanced material to ensure that advanced learners are not bored with the material and are being adequately challenged. Note that although students might advance quickly through some material, they should also be given time to delve more deeply into topics of interest at appropriate advanced levels of complexity and innovation.

Assessment is the way to determine the scope and degree of learning that has been mastered by the student. For purposes of gifted education, the assessments must be matched to differentiated outcomes, requiring the use of authentic approaches like performance- and portfolio-based assessment demands. Some assessments are already constructed and available for use, exhibiting strong technical adequacy and employed in research studies, whereas others may be teacher-developed, with opportunities to establish interrater reliability among teachers who may be using the assessments in schools. Care should be taken to use assessments that do not restrict the level of proficiency that students can demonstrate, such as above-grade-level assessments, and that allow for innovative and more complex responses.

Characteristics and needs of gifted learners is the basis for differentiating any curriculum area. Mathematically talented learners often have a strong number and computation sense, see relationships, recognize patterns, and make generalizations, and they may be highly fluent, flexible, and original at solving problems at an earlier stage of development than typical learners. Because of this advanced readiness, these students may need to be accelerated through the basic material in mathematics in order to focus on higher level math concepts and problems.

Complexity refers to a feature of differentiation that provides advanced learners more variables to study, asks them to use multiple resources to solve a problem, or requires them to use multiple higher order thinking skills simultaneously. The degree of complexity may depend on the developmental level of the learner, the nature of the learning task, and the readiness to take on the level of challenge required.

Creativity and innovation are used to suggest that activities conducted with the gifted employ opportunities for more open-ended project work that mirrors real-world professional work in solving problems in the disciplines. The terms also suggest that advanced learners are proficient in the skills and habits of mind associated with being a creator or innovator in a chosen field of endeavor. Thus, creative thinking and problem-solving skills would be emphasized.

Curriculum is a set of planned learning experiences, delineated from a framework of expectations at the goal or outcome level, that represent important knowledge, skills, and concepts to be learned. Differentiated curriculum units of study have already been designed and tested for effectiveness in mathematics, or units may be developed by teachers to use in gifted instruction.

Differentiation of curriculum for gifted learners is the process of adapting and modifying curriculum structures to address these learners' characteristics and needs more optimally. Curriculum goals, outcomes, and activities may be tailored for gifted learners to accommodate their needs. Typically, this process involves the use of the strategies of acceleration, complexity, depth, and creativity in combination.

Instruction is the delivery system for teaching that comprises the deliberate use of models, strategies, and supportive management techniques. For gifted learners, inquiry strategies such as Problem-Based Learning (PBL), Creative Problem Solving (CPS) and problem posing, and critical thinking models such as Paul's Reasoning Model used in independent research or within a flexible grouping approach in the regular classroom constitute instructional differentiation.

Rigor and relevance suggest that the curriculum experiences planned for advanced learners be sufficiently challenging yet provided in real-world or curricular contexts that matter to learners at their particular stage of development.

Talent trajectory is used to describe the school span development of advanced learners in their area of greatest aptitude from K–16. It is linked to developmental stages from early childhood through adolescence and defines key interventions that aid in the talent development process, specific to the subject area and desired career path.

Teacher quality refers to the movement at all levels of education to improve the knowledge base and skills of classroom teachers at P–12 levels, which is necessary for effective instruction for advanced students. It is the basis for a redesign of teacher education standards and a rationale for examining P–12 student outcomes in judging the efficacy of higher education programs for teachers. Policy makers are committed to this issue in improving our P–16 education programs.

Appendix B
Evidence-Based Practices
in Gifted Education

Evidence-based practices that inform the Teacher Preparation and Programming Standards in Gifted Education relate to assessment, curriculum, instruction, and grouping issues, all of which are embedded within the Common Core State Standards. These practices have an extensive research base. (The full references for the following citations can be found in the research base that accompanies the NAGC–CEC Teacher Preparation Standards in Gifted Education, available online at http://www.nagc.org.)

Assessment of Individual Characteristics and Needs
- Because of their advanced cognitive functioning, internal locus of control, motivation, and talents, teachers need to provide intellectual challenge in their classrooms to gifted and talented students (Ablard & Tissot, 1998; Barnett & Durden, 1993; Carter, 1985; Gross, 2000; McLauglin & Saccuzzo, 1997; Robinson & Clinkenbeard, 1998; Swiatek, 1993).
- Educators must also be receptive to gifted students' affective needs and sensitive to the socioemotional and coping needs of special groups of learners (e.g., highly

gifted, gifted students with disabilities, gifted students from diverse backgrounds, gifted girls, gifted boys; Albert & Runco, 1989; Coleman, 2001; Cross, Stewart, & Coleman, 2003; Ford & Harris, 2000; Gross, 2003; Kennedy, 1995; Peterson, 2003; Shaunessy & Self, 1998; Swiatek & Dorr, 1998).

- Gifted students' cultural, linguistic, and intellectual differences should be considered when planning instruction and differentiating curriculum (Boothe & Stanley, 2004).

- Educators need to use preassessment and ongoing assessment to adjust instruction that is consistent with the individual student's progress (Reis, Burns, & Renzulli, 1992; Winebrenner, 2003).

- Assessments used to document academic growth include authentic tasks, portfolios, and rubrics and performance-based assessments (Sheffield, 2003; Siegle, 2002; Treffinger, 1994; VanTassel-Baska, 2002).

- The results of progress assessments can be used to adjust instruction, including placement in appropriate group learning settings and academic acceleration (Feldhusen, 1996; Kulik, 1992).

Instruction

- Teachers need to use metacognitive and higher level thinking strategies in the content areas, activities that address the gifted students' areas of interest and foster research skills (Anderson & Krathwohl, 2001; Center for Gifted Education, 2000; Elder & Paul, 2003; Hébert, 1993; Johnsen & Goree, 2005; Moon, Feldhusen, & Dillon, 1994; VanTassel-Baska, Avery, Little, & Hughes, 2000).

- Educators should develop gifted students' use of cognitive strategies and encourage deliberate training in specific talent areas (Bloom & Sosniak, 1981; Ericcson & Charness, 1994; Feldman, 2003).

- Technology can be used in independent studies to access mentors and electronic resources and to enroll in advanced classes (Cross, 2004; Ravaglia, Suppes, Stillinger, & Alper, 1995; Siegle, 2004).

Curriculum

- In the classroom, curricular modifications for gifted students include acceleration, enrichment, grouping, Problem-Based Learning, curriculum compacting, tiered lessons, independent study, and specific curriculum models (Betts & Neihart, 1986; Brody, 2004; Colangelo, Assouline, & Gross, 2004; Gallagher & Stepien, 1996; Gavin, Casa, Adelson, Carroll, & Sheffield, 2009; Gavin & Sheffield, 2010; Gentry, 1999; Johnsen & Goree, 2005; Kulik & Kulik, 1992; Milgram, Hong, Shavit, & Peled, 1997; Renzulli & Reis, 2004; Rogers, 2003; Southern & Jones, 1991; Tomlinson, 2002; Tomlinson, Kaplan, Renzulli, Burns, Leppien, & Purcell, 2001; VanTassel-Baska & Little, 2003).
- Models emphasize the need for considering students' interests, environmental and natural catalysts, curriculum differentiation, and the development of higher level thinking skills (Elder & Paul, 2003; Gagné, 1995; Renzulli & Reis, 2003; Tomlinson & Cunningham-Eidson, 2003).
- When designing a differentiated curriculum, it is essential to develop a scope and sequence and align national, state or provincial, and/or local curricular standards with the differentiated curriculum (Maker, 2004; VanTassel-Baska & Johnsen, 2007; VanTassel-Baska & Stambaugh, 2006; Tassell, Stobaugh, Fleming, & Harper, 2010).
- Specific curricula have been designed for gifted students and include affective education, leadership, domain-specific studies, and the arts (Clark & Zimmerman, 1997; Nugent, 2005; Parker & Begnaud, 2003; VanTassel-Baska, 2003a).

- Educators should integrate academic and career guidance into learning plans for gifted students, particularly those from diverse backgrounds (Cline & Schwartz, 2000; Ford & Harris, 1997).
- Differentiated curricula results in increased student engagement, enhanced reasoning skills, and improved habits of mind (VanTassel-Baska, Avery, Little, & Hughes, 2000).
- When individuals from diverse backgrounds are provided challenging curricula, their abilities and potential are more likely to be recognized (Ford, 1996; Ford & Harris, 1997; Mills, Stork, & Krug, 1992).

Environment
- Working in groups with other gifted students and mentors can yield academic benefits and enhance self-confidence and communication skills (Brody, 1999; Davalos & Haensly, 1997; Grybe, 1997; Pleiss & Feldhusen, 1995; Torrance, 1984).
- Working under a successful mentor in an area of interest can foster personal growth, leadership skills, and high levels of learning (Betts, 2004; Brody, 1999; Davalos & Haensly, 1997; Feldhusen & Kennedy, 1988; Grybe, 1997; Pleiss & Feldhusen, 1995; Torrance, 1984).
- Other learning situations that support self-efficacy, creativity, and life-long learning include early college entrance programs, talent searches, math clubs and circles, online and afterschool/summer programs, competitions, Problem-Based Learning, independent play, independent study, and the International Baccalaureate program (Betts, 2004; Boothe, Sethna, Stanley, & Colgate, 1999; Christophersen & Mortweet, 2003; Gallagher, 1997; Johnsen & Goree, 2005; Karp, 2010; Olszewski-Kubilius, 1998; Poelzer & Feldhusen, 1997; Riley & Karnes, 1998; Rotigel & Lupkowski-Shoplik,

1999; Ruszcyk, 2012; Warshauer, McCabe, Sorto, Strickland, Warshauer, & White, 2010).

- Three factors need to be present for students to develop their talents: (a) above-average ability and motivation; (b) school, community, and/or family support; and (c) acceptance by peers in the domain of talent (Bloom, 1985; Csikszentmihalyi, 1996; Gagné, 2003; Renzulli, 1994; Siegle & McCoach, 2005).

Appendix C
Annotated References on Mathematical Creativity and Giftedness

Ablard, K. E., Mills, C. J., & Duvall, R. (1994). *Acceleration of CTY math and science students* (Tech. Rep. No. 10). Baltimore, MD: Johns Hopkins University, Center for Talented Youth.
Abstract: Varied types of acceleration, including individually paced precalculus and fast-paced science courses from the Center for Talented Youth and diagnostic-prescriptive approaches, were examined and student perceptions discussed. Students felt that acceleration was overall positive but felt isolated from their peers and uncomfortable being in classes with older students. However, students felt that the opportunity to be challenged outweighed the social negatives.

Ablard, K. E., & Tissot, S. L. (1998). Young students' readiness for advanced math: Precocious abstract reasoning. *Journal for the Education of the Gifted, 21,* 206–223.
Abstract: This study examined above-grade-level abstract reasoning abilities of 150 academically talented students ranging from grades 2–6. The School and College Ability Tests and the Arlin Test of Formal Reasoning were administered to each student. Understanding of various abstract concepts varied by age for only four of the eight subscales: probability, proportion, momentum,

and frames of references. In general, the students performed like students who were four grade levels higher. Those in third grade performed at five grade levels higher. The authors conclude that there may not be one age at which children acquire abstract reasoning. Gifted students are ready for advanced mathematics at a much earlier age.

Assouline, S. G., & Lupkowski-Shoplik, A. E. (2011). *Developing math talent: A comprehensive guide to math education for gifted students in elementary and middle school* (2nd ed.) Waco, TX: Prufrock Press.

Abstract: The authors provide concrete suggestions for identifying mathematically talented students, tools for instructional planning, and specific programming approaches. This updated second edition features topics such as strategies for identifying mathematically gifted learners, strategies for advocating for gifted children with math talent, how to design a systematic math education program for gifted students, specific curricula and materials that support success, and teaching strategies and approaches that encourage and challenge gifted learners.

Barbeau, E., & Taylor, P. J. (Eds.). (2009). *Challenging mathematics in and beyond the classroom: The 16th ICMI Study*. New York, NY: Springer.

Abstract: The last two decades have seen significant innovation both in classroom teaching and in the public presentation of mathematics. Much of this has centered on the use of games, puzzles, and investigations designed to capture interest, challenge the intellect, and encourage a more robust understanding of mathematical ideas and processes. ICMI Study 16 was commissioned to review these developments and describe experiences around the globe in different contexts, systematize the area, examine the effectiveness of the use of challenges, and set the stage for future study and development. A prestigious group of international researchers, with collective experience with national and international contests, classroom and general contests, and finding a place for mathematics in the public arena, contributed to this effort. The book deals with challenges for both gifted and regular students and with building public interest in appreciation of mathematics.

Babaeva, J. D. (1999). A dynamic approach to giftedness: Theory and practice. *High Ability Studies, 10,* 51–68.

Abstract: The aims of this research were to investigate the possibilities of developing the cognitive and creative abilities of recognized gifted children, and of raising the development of "ordinary" children up to a level of giftedness. This experimental work, based on Vygotsky's Dynamic Theory of Giftedness, involved special procedures and an experimental curriculum designed to overcome children's psychological barriers to learning. Five school classes were involved: three experimental classes, two of these gifted and one of average-ability children. Two further control classes were taught by conventional methods. Comparative assessments were made for 6 years between all the children, regarding cognitive development, creativity, and social giftedness, revealing considerable undeveloped potential of "ordinary" children. Major factors influencing IQ changes included the differences in psychological mechanisms to overcome barriers to learning. Due to the experimental psychological curriculum, not only did all the children's cognitive abilities increase, but also their creativity. Hence, these new diagnostic and developmental procedures were found to be effective, demonstrating the high practical value of the Dynamic Theory of Giftedness.

Barnett, L. B., & Durden, W. G. (1993). Education patterns of academically talented youth. *Gifted Child Quarterly, 37,* 161–168.

Abstract: In this study, 228 seventh-grade students who participated in the Johns Hopkins University Center for Talented Youth (CTY) Academic Programs were compared to 186 eligible seventh-grade students who did not enroll in CTY courses. The researchers used an ex post facto survey method to collect their data. They found that both groups were very successful academically in high school. Both took Advanced Placement and accelerated coursework in a broad range of disciplines and received high scores. They also distinguished themselves in extracurricular activities and graduated with distinction. However, the key differences between the groups related to their pursuit of a more challenging high school curriculum, results of standardized achievement tests, and college admission. The CTY group pursued calculus, took college courses earlier, and had a higher proportion of students who accelerated in subject areas.

Brody, L. (2004). *Grouping and acceleration practices in gifted education*. Thousand Oaks, CA: Corwin Press.
Abstract: This volume of seminal articles on grouping and acceleration emphasize the importance of flexibility when assigning students to instructional groups, modifying the groups when necessary. Grouping and acceleration have proved to be viable tools to differentiate content for students with different learning needs based on cognitive abilities and achievement levels.

Cahan, S., & Linchevski, L. (1996). The cumulative effect of ability grouping on mathematical achievement: A longitudinal perspective. *Studies in Educational Evaluation, 22,* 29–40.
Abstract: The regression-discontinuity design was used to study the cumulative effect of ability grouping in mathematics in Israeli junior high schools. Results from a final sample of 1,169 seventh graders show that placement in ability groups increases the gap between students at different grade levels.

Charlton, J. C., Marolf, D. M., & Stanley, J. C. (1994). Follow-up insights on rapid educational acceleration. *Roeper Review, 17,* 123–128.
Abstract: Two young adults who had participated in the Study of Mathematically Precocious Youth shared the effects of an accelerated program on their future. One graduate is an assistant professor of astrophysics at Pennsylvania State University

who received her Ph.D. in astrophysics from the University of Chicago at age 22. The other completed his Ph.D. in physics at the University of Texas at age 20. They believe that rapid progress through school grades all the way to the Ph.D. level is the optimal way for persons like themselves to enrich their educational experience and career.

Colangelo, N., Assouline, S. G., & Gross, M. U. M. (Eds.). (2004). *A nation deceived: How schools hold back America's brightest students* (Vol. 2). Iowa City: The University of Iowa, The Connie Belin & Jacqueline N. Blank International Center for Gifted Education and Talent Development. (Available at http://www.accelerationinstitute.org/Nation_Deceived/ Get_Report.aspx)

Abstract: Interviewed years later, an overwhelming majority of accelerated students say that acceleration was an excellent experience for them. They feel academically challenged and socially accepted, and they do not fall prey to the boredom that plagues many highly capable students who are forced to follow the curriculum for their age-peers. In spite of rich research evidence, schools, parents, and teachers have not accepted the idea of acceleration. *A Nation Deceived* presents the reasons that schools hold back America's brightest kids and shows that these reasons are simply not supported by research.

Gavin, M. K., Casa, T., Adelson, J. L., Carroll, S. R., & Sheffield, L. J. (2009). The impact of advanced curriculum on the achievement of mathematically promising students. *Gifted Child Quarterly, 53,* 188–202.

Abstract: This article describes the development of *Project M³: Mentoring Mathematical Minds* and reports on mathematics achievement results for students in grades 3–5 from 11 urban and suburban schools after exposure to the curriculum. Data analyses indicate statistically significant differences favoring each of the experimental groups over the comparison group on the

Iowa Tests of Basic Skills Concepts and Estimation Test and on Open-Response Assessments at all three grade levels.

Gavin, M. K., Casa, T. M., Adelson, J. L., Carroll, S. R., Sheffield, L. J., & Spinelli, A. M. (2007). Project M[3]: Mentoring Mathematical Minds: A research-based curriculum for talented elementary students. *Journal of Advanced Academics, 18,* 566–585.

Abstract: To date, there has been very little research-based mathematics curriculum available for talented elementary students. Yet the gifted education and mathematics literature suggest support for curriculum that is both enriched and accelerated with a focus on developing conceptual understanding and mathematical thinking. Project M[3]: Mentoring Mathematical Minds is a 5-year Javits research grant project designed to create curriculum units with these essential elements for talented elementary students. These units combine exemplary teaching practices of gifted education with the content and process standards promoted by the National Council of Teachers of Mathematics. The content at each level is at least one to two grade levels above the regular curriculum and includes number and operations, algebra, geometry and measurement, and data analysis and probability. The focus of the pedagogy is encouraging students to act as practicing professionals by emphasizing verbal and written communication. Research was conducted on the implementation of 12 units in 11 different schools, nine in Connecticut and two in Kentucky. The sample consisted of approximately 200 mathematically talented students entering third grade, with most remaining in the project through fifth grade. More than 40% of students were eligible for meal subsidies, and the sample was composed of students from diverse racial and ethnic groups. Paired t-tests were conducted on the total scores for each unit pre- and posttest. Changes in the total scores for each unit indicated statistically significant gains from pretest mean to posttest mean at the $p < .01$ level of statistical significance. In addition, the effect sizes were all large and ranged from 1.55 to 3.49. These results indicate significant increases in understanding across all mathematical concepts in each unit from pre- to posttesting. Thus, Project M³ materials may help fill a curriculum void by providing appropriate accelerated and enriched units to meet the needs of talented elementary students.

Gross, M. U. M. (2006). Exceptionally gifted children: Long-term outcomes of academic acceleration and nonacceleration. *Journal for the Education of the Gifted, 29,* 40–429.
Abstract: The 20-year longitudinal study traced the academic, social, and emotional development of 60 young Australians with IQs of 160 and above. The 60 youth were spread over Australia with 7 of the youth living overseas. To be included in the study, the youth needed to be between the ages of 5 and 13 in the years 1988–1989. The majority of the youth who had been radically accelerated or who were accelerated by 2 years reported high degrees of life satisfaction, have taken research degrees at leading universities, have professional careers, and report facilitative social and love relationships. Youth of equal abilities who were accelerated by only one year or who were not permitted to accelerate have entered less academically rigorous college courses, reported lower levels of life satisfaction, and experienced significant difficulties with socialization. The author concluded with two primary recommendations. First, students should not only accelerate in their areas of special talent but should also be allowed to explore possible pathways of other talent areas. Second, exceptionally gifted students should be identified early and accelerated or placed in a class with other gifted children.

Johnsen, S. (2005). Within-class acceleration. *Gifted Child Today, 28*(1), 5.
Abstract: This article describes ways teachers can accelerate the curriculum in their classrooms by preassessing students and modifying their instruction, allowing them either to move through the curriculum at a faster pace or to provide in-depth learning experiences.

Kolitch, E. R., & Brody, L. E. (1992). Mathematics acceleration of highly talented students: An evaluation. *Gifted Child
Quarterly, 36,* 78–86.
Abstract: Approximately 750 students who had participated in
the Study of Mathematically Precocious Youth responded to a
questionnaire regarding the effects of the program. These students did well in mathematics courses taken several years earlier
than is typical and excelled on AP calculus examinations. The
majority of the students took calculus 2 1/2 years earlier. The
students also participated in mathematics competitions and summer programs, reported working with mentors, became involved
in independent projects, and read mathematics books on their
own. In general, the females appeared to be less likely to accelerate greatly.

Leikin, R., Berman, A., & Koichu, B. (Eds.). (2009). *Creativity
in mathematics and the education of gifted students.* Rotterdam,
the Netherlands: Sense.
Abstract: This book suggests directions for closing the gap
between research in the field of mathematics education and
research in the field of creativity and giftedness. It also outlines
a research agenda for further research and development in the
field. The book consists of a balanced set of chapters by mathematicians, mathematics educators, educational physiologists, and
educational researchers. The authors of different chapters accept
a dynamic conception of creativity and giftedness. The book provides analysis of cognitive, affective, and social factors associated
with the development of creativity in all students and with the
realization of mathematical talent in gifted students. It contains
theoretical essays, research reports, historical overviews, recommendations for curricular design, and insights about promotion
of mathematical creativity and giftedness at different levels. The
readers will find many examples of challenging mathematical
problems intended for developing or examining mathematical
creativity and giftedness, as well as ideas for direct implementation in school and tertiary mathematics courses. They will also

find theoretical models that can be used in researching students' creativity and giftedness. Research reports enlighten relationships between excellence in mathematics and creativity and examine different aspects of an inquiry-based environment as a powerful way for developing mathematical creativity in school students.

Lubinski, D., & Benbow, C. P. (1995). The Study of Mathematically Precocious Youth: The first three decades of a planned 50-year study of intellectual talent. In R. F. Subotnik & K. D. Arnold (Eds.), *Beyond Terman: Contemporary longitudinal studies of giftedness and talent* (pp. 255–289). Norwood, NJ: Ablex.
Abstract: This longitudinal study outlines a diagnostic-prescriptive talent development acceleration program in mathematics through Johns Hopkins University. Positive effects using this approach have been documented.

Lupkowski-Shoplik, A. E., & Assouline, S. G. (1994). Evidence of extreme mathematical precocity: Case studies of talented youths. *Roeper Review, 16,* 144–151.

Abstract: This article describes four extraordinarily talented youngsters, two boys and two girls, who demonstrate an "uncanny" understanding of mathematics. By the time that Steve was 6 1/2 years old, he could solve algebra problems, type 50 words a minute, and write his own computer programs. By the age of 3, Peter could count more than 20 objects accurately, read numbers past 1,000, read silently, calculate sums and differences of numbers less than 10, and play nursery songs on his xylophone accurately. By the time Joanna was 2 1/2, she was adding and subtracting Cheerios® at breakfast. Besides having early mathematical problem solving ability, Lisa read fluently by the time she was 3 1/2 and had learned all of the basic operations in mathematics when she was 6 years old. Given the difficulty that the parents encountered in attempting to find appropriate programming in public school, the researchers made some of these suggestions: Parents should be advocates for their children, have their child tested using standardized testing, and find enrichment programs outside the school system. Assessments should identify skills and content that the children already know so they might be challenged in school. Acceleration should be balanced with the study of other academic subjects and extracurricular activities. Talented students need to find an intellectual peer group.

Mann, E. L. (2006). Creativity: The essence of mathematics. *Journal for the Education of the Gifted, 30,* 236–262.
Abstract: For the gifted mathematics student, early mastery of concepts and skills in the mathematics curriculum usually results in getting more of the same work and/or moving through the curriculum at a faster pace. Testing, grades, and pacing overshadow the essential role of creativity involved in doing mathematics. Talent development requires creative applications in the exploration of mathematics problems. Traditional teaching methods involving demonstration and practice using closed problems with predetermined answers insufficiently prepare students in mathematics. Students leave school with adequate computational skills but lack the ability to apply these skills in meaningful ways. Teaching mathematics without providing for creativity denies all students, especially gifted and talented students, the opportunity to appreciate the beauty of mathematics and fails to provide the gifted student an opportunity to fully develop his or her talents. In this article, a review of literature defines mathematical creativity, develops an understanding of the creative student of mathematics, and discusses the issues and implications for the teaching of mathematics.

Mills, C. J., & Ablard, K. E. (1993). Credit and placement for academically talented students following special summer courses in math and science. *Journal for the Education of the Gifted, 17,* 4–25.
Abstract: The researchers surveyed 892 academically talented students about academic credit and/or course placement for their

participation in a precalculus or fast-paced science course during the summer. They found that 39% of the math students received credit and 38% of the science students received credit in their schools.

Mills, C. J., Ablard, K. E., & Lynch, S. J. (1992). Academically talented students' preparation for advanced-level coursework after individually-paced precalculus class. *Journal for the Education of the Gifted, 16,* 3–17.

Abstract: These researchers found that intensive summer precalculus mathematics courses that allowed students to proceed at an individual pace provided greater challenge and the prerequisites necessary to succeed in subsequent mathematics courses. About 80% of the students reported having received a grade of A in their high school mathematics course despite the fact that many were one or more years younger than their classmates. The authors conclude that schools should not be concerned that fast-paced courses do not adequately prepare gifted students for more advanced courses.

Miller, R., Mills, C., & Tangherlini, A. (1995). The Appalachia Model Mathematics Program for gifted students. *Roeper Review, 18,* 138–141.

Abstract: In this study, 456 students in grades 2–6 participated in the model mathematics program. The students were placed in four instructional groups on the basis of their quantitative scores on The School and College Ability Test. Each student in the MMP received an individual education plan, and assessments were administered to determine mathematics placement within the curriculum. In 3 months, students in Group 4 (the fastest paced) mastered 1.3 years of content; students in Group 3 mastered 1.0 years; and students in Group 2 mastered .4 years. The majority of Groups 3 and 4 were ready for algebra by seventh grade. A number of the students completed the high school mathematics course offerings as early as ninth grade. More students also participated in the Johns Hopkins University Talent Search and increased their performance on the SAT math.

Miserandino, A. D., Subotnik, R. F., & Kenrick, O. (1995).
Identifying and nurturing mathematical talent in urban
school settings. *The Journal of Secondary Gifted Education, 6,*
245–257.
Abstract: This article is a summary of the results of a 3-year Javits
grant that was designed to identify and nurture science and mathematical talent. Forty-five participants from an inner city high
school, a heterogeneous magnet school, a laboratory high school,
and an elementary school for the gifted were involved in the
study. Together with their teacher-mentors, the students spent
10 six-hour days studying and exploring advanced mathematical concepts in number theory, fractals, and probability by way
of workshops offered by Hunter College mathematics profes-
sors and by teacher-mentors. Students also visited metropolitan
area exhibits on mathematics-related topics. Results indicated
that students increased confidence in their mathematical skills
and selected more advanced mathematics courses in their high
schools. The presence of a mentor proved to be a critical factor
in motivating students to take advanced courses.

Olszewski-Kubilius, P., & Yasumoto, J. (1995). Factors affecting
the academic choices of academically talented middle school
students. *Journal for the Education of the Gifted, 18,* 298–318.
Abstract: Using a sample of 656 middle school students who
participated in a summer academic program, researchers found
that gender influences the selection of math and science courses
over verbal ones. Parental attitudes, previous educational experiences, and ethnicity (in this study Asian American) influenced
the selection of math and science courses over verbal courses.
The importance that parents place on mathematics and science
for their child's future may have the most powerful influence on
a child's selection of mathematics and science courses.

Ravaglia, R., Suppes, P., Stillinger, C., & Alper, T. M. (1995).
Computer-based mathematics and physics for gifted students. *Gifted Child Quarterly, 39,* 7–13.

Abstract: A group of 27 middle and high school students took computer-based advanced math classes at a middle school. A tutor provided assistance that included correcting offline work, grading tests, and certifying performance in the course. Ninety-two percent of those who took Calculus AB (the first two quarters of college calculus), 100% of those who took Calculus BC (the entire year of college calculus), and 88% of those who took Physics C received scores of 4 or 5 on Advanced Placement tests. The computer courses were designed at the Education Program for Gifted Youth (EPGY) at Stanford University. The authors concluded that computer-based education makes it possible for gifted and talented middle and early high school students to complete advanced courses in mathematics and physics earlier than expected.

Reis, S. M., & Park, S. (2001). Gender differences in high-achieving students in math and science. *Journal for the Education of the Gifted, 25,* 52–73.

Abstract: Using data from the National Education Longitudinal Study of 1988, the researchers examined gender differences between high-achieving students in math and science. They found that there were more high-achieving males than females in this group, with far fewer female students in the science group. They also found that high-achieving males felt better about themselves than high-achieving females. Females who are high-achieving in math and science are more influenced than males are by teachers and families.

Robinson, N. M., Abbot, R. D., Berninger, V. W., Busse, J., & Mukhopadhyay, S. (1997). Developmental changes in mathematically precocious young children: Longitudinal and gender effects. *Gifted Child Quarterly, 41,* 145–158.

Abstract: Young children with advanced mathematical skill ($N = 276$) were followed for 2 years during kindergarten through first grade or first through second grade. Children were randomly assigned to a control group or a treatment group. Children in the treatment group participated in enrichment activities outside the school that supplemented the child's regular classroom program. Activities were problem-based and "constructivist" in nature. The students were administered the Stanford-Binet IV, Key Math Test-Revised, Woodcock-Johnson Achievement Test-Revised, and the Word Problems Test. Gains occurred on three of the five math subtests, two of the three verbal subtests, and both visual-spatial subtests, with maintenance on the remaining three standardized subtests. Children who are advanced in math early continue to be advanced and may become more advanced relative to age peers once they enter school. Boys surpassed girls in performance. The intervention resulted in change in the quantitative domain but not the verbal or visual-spatial domains.

Saul, M., Assouline, S. G., & Sheffield, L. J. (Eds.). (2010). *The peak in the middle: Developing mathematically gifted students in the middle grades.* Reston, VA: National Council of Teachers of Mathematics.
Abstract: Good teaching is responsive to individual differences, tailoring instruction to meet the needs of individual learners. In gifted education, students need a curriculum that is differentiated (by level, complexity, breadth, and depth), developmentally appropriate, and conducted at an appropriate developmental level. This collection of essays from experts in the field addresses the particular needs educational institutions have in serving their gifted students. Topics include policy and philosophy, specific program models, supplemental materials and programs, knowledge and skills that teachers need in their work, international opportunities and possibilities, and equity. Many of the points raised are as valid for general education students as they are for gifted students. Many relate equally well to high school or elementary school. And many apply across the curriculum—not just to mathematics.

Sheffield, L. J. (2003). *Extending the challenge in mathematics: Developing mathematical promise in K–8 students.* Thousand Oaks, CA: Corwin Press.

Abstract: This book is a guide to the development of mathematical talent in students in grades K–8. The first chapter is on developing mathematical promise and considers characteristics of students who are mathematically promising, the goals of mathematics instruction, how to find and/or create good problems, models for increasing the numbers and levels of mathematically promising students, and assessment strategies. The remaining chapters offer suggested investigations into the following subject areas: number and operations, algebra, geometry and measurement, and data analysis and probability. Investigations offer activities at three levels of difficulty and are based on an open problem-solving heuristic.

Sheffield, L. J. (Ed.). (1999). *Developing mathematically promising students*. Reston, VA: National Council of Teachers of Mathematics.

Abstract: This book, written on the recommendation of the Task Force on Mathematically Promising Students, investigates issues involving the development of promising mathematics students. Recommendations are made concerning topics such as the definition of promising students; the identification of such students; appropriate curriculum, instruction, and assessment; cultural influences; teacher preparation and enhancement; and appropriate next steps.

Sowell, E. J. (1993). Programs for mathematically gifted students: A review of empirical research. *Gifted Child Quarterly, 37,* 124–132.

Abstract: This article summarizes and critiques the empirical research on programs for mathematically gifted students. The research indicates that accelerating the mathematics curriculum is desirable for the precocious student who reasons well. Precocious students enjoy working with others who are precocious and find the fast pace "invigorating." Because definitions of mathematical enrichment are unclear, the author found it impossible to draw conclusions about its efficacy.

Sriraman, B. (Ed.). (2008). *Creativity, giftedness, and talent development in mathematics.* Charlotte, NC: Information Age.
Abstract: Given the lack of research-based perspectives on talent development in mathematics education, this monograph is specifically focused on contributions toward the constructs of creativity and giftedness in mathematics. This monograph presents new perspectives for talent development in the mathematics classroom and gives insights into the psychology of creativity and giftedness. The book is aimed at classroom teachers, coordinators of gifted programs, math contest coaches, graduate students, and researchers interested in creativity, giftedness, and talent development in mathematics.

Sriraman, B., & Lee, K. H. (Eds.). (2011). *The elements of creativity and giftedness in mathematics.* Rotterdam, the Netherlands: Sense.
Abstract: This book covers recent advances in mathematics education pertaining to the development of creativity and giftedness. The book is international in scope in the sense that it includes numerous studies on mathematical creativity and giftedness conducted in the U.S., China, Korea, Turkey, Israel, Sweden, and Norway in addition to cross-national perspectives from Canada and Russia. The topics include problem-posing, problem-solving, and mathematical creativity; the development of mathematical creativity with students, preservice teachers, and in-service teachers; cross-cultural views of creativity and giftedness; the unpacking of notions and labels such as high achieving, inclusion, and potential; and the theoretical state of the art on the constructs of mathematical creativity and giftedness.

Swiatek, M. A. (1993). A decade of longitudinal research on academic acceleration through the Study of Mathematically Precocious Youth. *Roeper Review, 15,* 120–123.
Abstract: Five cohorts who participated in the Johns Hopkins University Study of Mathematically Precocious Youth were surveyed at the age of 19, some at the age of 23, and some at the age

of 33. Students who choose to accelerate in high school do not suffer academically but gain speed in their educational preparation. These students perform well at advanced levels of study, complete college, and attend graduate school in numbers that exceed the national average. In addition, the students also express satisfaction with college and their experiences.

VanTassel-Baska, J. (Ed.). (2004). *Curriculum for gifted and talented students*. Thousand Oaks, CA: Corwin Press.
Abstract: A collection of seminal articles and research from *Gifted Child Quarterly* are compiled in one volume, including articles on how to develop a scope and sequence for the gifted, the multiple menu model of serving gifted students, what effective curriculum for the gifted looks like, curriculum at the secondary level, and specific content-area curricula options in math and science.

Vogeli, B. R. (1997). *Special secondary schools for the mathematically and scientifically talented: An international panorama*. New York, NY: Columbia University Teachers College.
Abstract: This is a 284-page report on special schools for the mathematically and scientifically talented. These schools are one manifestation of concern for the identification and development of an important world resource—the gifted youth of every nation. Despite proliferation of special schools, information about them is widely dispersed in professional journals, news reports, and advertising literature prepared by the schools themselves. This report, which describes more than 50 special schools in 12 nations, is intended neither as a comparative study nor as an in-depth analysis of individual schools, but rather as an "international guidebook"—a ready reference for the educator, politician, philanthropist, or parent concerned with the education of the gifted.

Appendix D
Additional Mathematics Resources

Assouline, S. G., & Lupkowski-Shoplik, A. (2011). *Developing math talent: A comprehensive guide to math education for gifted students in elementary and middle school* (2nd ed.). Waco, TX: Prufrock Press.

Blackwell, L., Trzesniewski, K. H., & Dweck, C. S. (2007). Implicit theories of intelligence predict achievement across an adolescent transition: A longitudinal study and an intervention. *Child Development, 78,* 246–263.

Bossé, M., & Rotigel, J. (2006). *Encouraging your child's mathematical talent: The involved parent's guide.* Waco, TX: Prufrock Press.

Chamberlin, S. A. (2005). Secondary mathematics for high-ability students. In F. A. Dixon & S. M. Moon (Eds.), *The handbook of secondary gifted education* (pp. 145–163). Waco, TX: Prufrock Press.

Chamberlin, S. A. (2012). *Serving the needs of intellectually advanced mathematics students K–6.* Marion, IL: Pieces of Learning.

Chamberlin, S. A. (in press). *Using model-eliciting activities to investigate concepts in statistics.* Waco, TX: Prufrock Press.

Dweck, C. (2006). *Mindset: The new psychology of success.* New York, NY: Random House.

Gardiner, T. (2000). *Maths challenge.* Oxford, England: Oxford University Press.

Gavin, M. K. (2005, Fall/Winter). Are we missing anyone? Identifying mathematically promising students. *Gifted Education Communicator,* 24–29.

Gavin, M. K., & Adelson, J. L. (2008). Mathematics, elementary. In C. M. Callahan & J. Plucker (Eds.), *Critical issues and practices in gifted education: What the research says* (pp. 367–394). Waco, TX: Prufrock Press.

Gavin, M. K., Sheffield, L. J., & Chapin, S. (2011). *Math innovations: Moving math forward through critical thinking and exploration.* Dubuque, IA: Kendall Hunt.

Hanushek, E. A., Peterson, P. E., & Woessmann, L. (2010). *U.S. math performance in global perspective: How well does each state do at producing high-achieving students?* Boston, MA: Harvard Kennedy School.

Johnsen, S. K., & Kendrick, J. (2005). *Math education for gifted students.* Waco, TX: Prufrock Press.

Koshy, V. (2001). *Teaching mathematics to able children.* London, England: David Fulton.

Loveless, T., Farkas, S., & Duffet, A. (2008). *High-achieving students in the era of No Child Left Behind: Part 1: An analysis of NAEP data.* Washington, DC: Fordham Institute.

National Academy of Sciences. (2007). *Rising above the gathering storm: Energizing and employing America for a brighter economic future.* Washington, DC: The National Academies Press.

National Academy of Sciences. (2010). *Rising above the gathering storm, revisited: Rapidly approaching category 5.* Washington, DC: The National Academies Press.

National Center for Education Statistics. (2011). *The nation's report card: Mathematics 2011.* Retrieved from http://nces.ed.gov/nationsreportcard/pubs/main2011/2012458.asp

National Council of Supervisors of Mathematics. (2011). *Improving student achievement by expanding opportunities for our most promising students of mathematics.* Denver, CO: Author.

National Council of Teachers of Mathematics. (2006). *Curriculum focal points for prekindergarten through grade 8 mathematics.* Reston, VA: Author.

National Mathematics Advisory Panel. (2008). *Foundations for success: The final report of the National Mathematics Advisory Panel.* Retrieved from http://www2.ed.gov/about/bdscomm/list/mathpanel/report/final-report.pdf

Sowell, E. J., Bergwell, L., Zeigler, A. J., & Cartwright, R. M. (1990). Identification and description of mathematically gifted students: A review of empirical research. *Gifted Child Quarterly, 34,* 147–154.

Sriraman, B. (2003). Mathematical giftedness, problem solving, and the ability to formulate generalizations. *The Journal of Secondary Gifted Education, 14,* 151–165.

Tassell, J. L., Stobaugh, R. R., Fleming, B. D., & Harper, C. R. (2010). Articulation. In M. Saul, S. G. Assouline, & L. J. Sheffield (Eds.), *The peak in the middle: Developing mathematically gifted students in the middle grades* (pp. 115–132). Reston, VA: National Council of Teachers of Mathematics.

About the Editors

Susan K. Johnsen, Ph.D., is professor in the Department of Educational Psychology at Baylor University, where she directs the Ph.D. program and programs related to gifted and talented education. She is the author of more than 200 publications, including *Identifying Gifted Students: A Practical Guide*, books related to implementing the national teacher preparation standards in gifted education, and tests used in identifying gifted students, and is editor-in-chief of *Gifted Child Today*. She serves on the Board of Examiners of the National Council for Accreditation of Teacher Education, is a reviewer and auditor of programs in gifted education, and is chair of the Knowledge and Skills Subcommittee of the Council for Exceptional Children. She is past president of The Association for the Gifted (TAG) and past president of the Texas Association for the Gifted and Talented (TAGT).

Linda J. Sheffield, Ph.D., is Regents Professor Emerita of Mathematics Education at Northern Kentucky University and founding director of the Kentucky Center for Mathematics and is a coauthor of *Math Innovations*, a middle-grades mathematics series, as well as the Javits-funded *Project M³: Mentoring Mathematical Minds* and the NSF *Project M²: Mentoring Young Mathematicians,* two series of units for advanced elementary and primary students. Dr. Sheffield has authored, coauthored, or edited approximately 50 books and has conducted seminars for educators, parents, and students across the United States and in nearly 20 other countries with an emphasis on helping students develop their mathematical creativity, promise, talents, and abilities to the fullest extent possible. She a leader of the National Association for Gifted Children STEM Network and the National Council of Supervisors of Mathematics Special Interest Group on Mathematically Promising Students, was chair of the National Council of Teachers of Mathematics Task Force on Promising Students, and is past president of the School Science and Mathematics Association.

About the Contributors

Cheryll M. Adams, Ph.D., is the Director Emerita of the Center for Gifted Studies and Talent Development at Ball State University and teaches graduate courses for the license in gifted education. She has authored or coauthored numerous publications in professional journals, as well as several books and book chapters. She serves on the editorial review boards for *Roeper Review*, *Gifted Child Quarterly*, and *Journal for the Education of the Gifted*. She has served on the Board of Directors of the National Association for Gifted Children, has been president of the Indiana Association for the Gifted, and currently serves as president of The Association for the Gifted, Council for Exceptional Children.

Alicia Cotabish, Ed.D., is an assistant professor of teaching and learning at the University of Central Arkansas. Alicia directed STEM Starters, a Jacob K. Javits project, and was the former Associate Director of the Jodie Mahony Center for Gifted Education at the University of Arkansas at Little Rock. Her recent work has focused on STEM and gifted education, school administration, and low-income promising learners.

Chrystyna V. Mursky, Ph.D., is the State Director for Gifted and Talented, Advanced Placement, and International Baccalaureate in the Wisconsin Department of Public Instruction. She has been involved in education for more than 30 years and in gifted education for 18 years. As a classroom teacher, she taught science and math. In addition, she served as a gifted and talented resource teacher and K–12 coordinator in rural, suburban, and urban school districts in Wisconsin. Dr. Mursky holds bachelor's degrees in zoology and elementary education, a master's degree in curriculum and instruction, and a Ph.D. in educational policy and leadership.

Joyce VanTassel-Baska, Ed.D., is the Smith Professor Emerita at The College of William and Mary, where she developed a graduate program and a research and development center in gifted education. Formerly, she initiated and directed the Center for Talent Development at Northwestern University. She has also served as the state director of gifted programs for Illinois, as a regional director of a gifted service center in the Chicago area, as coordinator of gifted programs for the Toledo, OH, public school system, and as a teacher of gifted high school students in English and Latin. Dr. VanTassel-Baska has published widely, including 27 books and more than 500 refereed journal articles, book chapters, and scholarly reports. Her major research interests are the talent development process and effective curricular interventions with the gifted.

About the Copublishers

About NAGC

The National Association for Gifted Children (NAGC) is an organization of parents, teachers, educators, other professionals, and community leaders who unite to address the unique needs of children and youth with demonstrated gifts and talents as well as those children who may be able to develop their talent potential with appropriate educational experiences.

We support and develop policies and practices that encourage and respond to the diverse expressions of gifts and talents in children and youth from all cultures, racial and ethnic backgrounds, and socioeconomic groups. NAGC supports and engages in research and development, staff development, advocacy, communication, and collaboration with other organizations and agencies who strive to improve the quality of education for all students.

About NCSM

The National Council of Supervisors of Mathematics (NCSM) is a mathematics leadership organization for educational leaders that provides professional learning opportunities necessary to support and sustain improved student achievement.

NCSM envisions a professional and diverse learning community of educational leaders that ensures every student in every classroom has access to effective mathematics teachers, relevant curricula, culturally responsive pedagogy, and current technology.

To achieve our NCSM vision, we will:

N: Network and collaborate with stakeholders in education, business, and government communities to ensure the growth and development of mathematics education leaders

C: Communicate to mathematics leaders current and relevant research, and provide up-to-date information on issues, trends, programs, policies, best practices and technology in mathematics education

S: Support and sustain improved student achievement through the development of leadership skills and relationships among current and future mathematics leaders

M: Motivate mathematics leaders to maintain a life-long commitment to provide equity and access for all learners

NATIONAL COUNCIL OF
TEACHERS OF MATHEMATICS

About NCTM

The National Council of Teachers of Mathematics (NCTM) is a public voice of mathematics education, providing vision, leadership, and professional development to support teachers in ensuring mathematics learning of the highest quality for all students. With more than 80,000 members and 230 Affiliates, NCTM is the world's largest organization dedicated to improving mathematics education in prekindergarten through grade 12. The Council's *Principles and Standards for School Mathematics* includes guidelines for excellence in mathematics education and issues a call for all students to engage in more challenging mathematics. Its *Curriculum Focal Points for Prekindergarten through Grade 8 Mathematics* identifies the most important mathematical topics for each grade level. *Focus in High School Mathematics: Reasoning and Sense Making* advocates practical changes to the high school mathematics curriculum to refocus learning on reasoning and sense making. NCTM is dedicated to ongoing dialogue and constructive discussion with all stakeholders about what is best for our nation's students.

.